BKM KB.2

THE ANOINTING

G·K Hall &Co.

This Large Print Book carries the
Seal of Approval of N.A.V.H.

THE ANOINTING

Benny Hinn

G.K. Hall & Co.
Thorndike, Maine

Published in Large Print by arrangement with
Thomas Nelson Publishers, Inc.

G.K. Hall Large Print Book Series.

Set in 16 pt. News Plantin by Jan Cronkite.

Printed on acid free paper in the United States of America.

Library of Congress Cataloging-in-Publication Data

Hinn, Benny.
    The anointing / Benny Hinn.
      p. cm.—(G.K. Hall large print book series)
    ISBN 0-8161-5639-5 (alk. paper : lg. print)
    1. Spiritual life—Pentecostal churches. 2. Holy Spirit. 3. Gifts,
Spiritual. 4. Large type books. I. Title.
[BV4501.2.H494   1993]
248.4'.8994—dc20

                                         92-28732
                                            CIP

Dedicated to my son, Joshua. I pray
that he will carry God's message of
salvation and the power of the Holy Spirit
to the ends of the earth.

Special thanks go to Bob Slosser for his
professional help and editorial skills in
the development of this manuscript.

CONTENTS

Preface   9
1   Disaster in Detroit   11
2   The Most Valuable Gift   17
3   In the Beginning   24
4   An Answer at Last   37
5   It's Not By Might   58
6   An Unusual Woman of God   71
7   What Is It?   81
8   You Must Have It   90
9   Three Anointings   100
10 It Didn't Begin Yesterday   112
11 Jesus, the I AM   120
12 It's for You — Now   129
13 Two Profound Basics   137
14 The Example of Jesus   149
15 Change Your Oil   166
16 Getting a Double Portion   176
17 Will You Pay the Price?   187

Preface

In my previous book, *Good Morning, Holy Spirit,* I emphasized the reality of the Holy Spirit as God, an equal member of the Trinity, a person as real as, if not more so than, you or I. My purpose in that book was to acquaint you with the Spirit and to lead you into the experience of His presence.

My purpose in *The Anointing* is to further that beautiful, ongoing relationship and lead you into the reality of the power to serve the Lord Jesus in His particular calling on your life. The power is the anointing of the Holy Spirit as promised by Jesus after His resurrection: "Ye shall receive power, after that the Holy Ghost is come upon you; and ye shall be witnesses unto me" (Acts 1:8 KJV).

I think we all agree that if there ever was a time when the body of Christ needed power, this is it. Only the miracle-working power of Almighty God can roll back the tide of sin and disease flooding the world in every corner.

Weakness is not our inheritance as Christians, yet many of us have settled for just that. The Bible says our witness to Christ can be confirmed "with signs following" (Mark 18:20).

9

Fulfillment of that promise is the purpose of the anointing of the Spirit, and equipping you with this hidden treasure is the purpose of this book.

First there must be the presence, and then comes the anointing. The anointing is not the baptism of the Holy Spirit, although that is important. The anointing is the power, the power to serve God. You will know assuredly when the presence of the Holy Spirit has come upon your life, for you will have sweet fellowship. And you will know immediately when He has empowered you spiritually, mentally, and physically to battle demons and disease.

Make no mistake about it: God wants you to have these two great gifts. This will become real as you read on.

You have life-changing moments ahead. May the Lord bless you in every way as you go forward step by step. We serve a wonderful and powerful God!

Chapter 1

Disaster in Detroit

I lay on the bed in my Detroit hotel room and relaxed, praying quietly and worshiping the Lord. It was a Saturday night in 1980, the clock showed midnight, and I was to preach the next morning and evening at a church just outside of town.

After a few moments, the presence of God came into the room so strongly that tears began to roll down my face and I was caught up in His glory. The presence — that wonderful presence of the Holy Spirit that had so revolutionized my life several years earlier — was so heavy that I was oblivious to everything. Before I knew it, the time was 2 A.M., and I was still praying.

The next morning I rose quickly, feeling rested and strong, and prayed again before leaving for the service. I was aware that my prayer session this time was not extraordinary. It felt nothing like the night before, but that would have been hard to equal.

I went to the service and, when the time came,

11

began to preach. I opened my mouth to say the first words, and a cloud of glory came into that building. It was as though the shekinah — the awesome holy presence of God Almighty — glory had arrived. It was heavy — so heavy that you couldn't move.

People began to weep. As I was speaking, some fell from their seats onto the floor. They just crumbled and sobbed. Their response was amazing. What was happening?

Then I closed my eyes and said one word: Jesus.

Whoosh! God's presence and power swept through the auditorium even greater than before, and people everywhere were moved. I saw no one who wasn't touched visibly.

A man next to me said, "I've never felt God's presence like I'm feeling it now." Tears were streaming down his face.

I knew he was right. I had never before felt the presence and the anointing of the Holy Spirit so powerfully in a service.

A Break for Lunch

Following the service, I was scheduled to have lunch at the home of a cousin who lived in Detroit. I had not seen her in some time and looked forward to lunch with her.

My cousin and her husband welcomed me when I arrived, and we sat down at the table together as we renewed our acquaintance. We had a delightful lunch, and our conversation was lively and enjoyable.

Suddenly, as we sat enjoying our lunch, I felt the Lord tugging at my heart. I knew the feeling well. He was gently calling me: "Go pray."

I was startled, and in my heart I responded, *Lord, I can't leave now. I'm having lunch with these people. And I didn't even drive here myself. The hotel is forty-five minutes away, and I have no way to get there. Besides, how can I get up and leave in the middle of lunch?*

Silence.

Our lunch concluded, and the man who had driven me there took me back to the hotel. I was so exhausted when I got to my room that I took a nap.

When I arrived at the service that evening, the crowd was double what it had been in the morning. God's power had been so awesome that the people were still excited, filled with anticipation about the evening service. What would tonight be like if the morning meeting had been so powerful?

It Was Different

I got up to preach, but when I opened my mouth, there was nothing — only words. No presence. No overwhelming anointing of the Spirit. No power.

I struggled. I didn't know what to do next. I could tell by the expression on their faces that many were wondering what was going on. The truth was: *Nothing* was going on.

Only hours before, I had simply spoken the word *Jesus*, and God's power had invaded the auditorium. People had felt the touch of God as they wept in His presence. But now . . . I was saying everything I could think of, and nothing was happening.

Finally the service ended. It was a disaster!

I couldn't get back to my hotel room fast enough. I rushed into the room, closed the door quickly, and locked it. What a relief! The service had seemed like an eternity.

I sat on the bed, and my mind raced over the ordeal. I was puzzled and confused. "God, what happened? This morning Your presence was so overwhelming and Your power so great that I could barely stand in the midst of Your glory. People were moved to tears."

The words continued to pour out of me. "It was like heaven. But tonight! What was wrong? Why did the service seem so empty? So empty of You?" Finally I stopped. And the soft, gentle voice of the Holy Spirit whispered, "Remember this afternoon when I was tugging at you, saying, 'Go pray'? You chose to stay with your cousin. You gave your cousin and her husband the place that belongs to Me. You put them before Me."

Much quieter, but very defensive, I responded, "But, Lord, I couldn't leave. What would my cousin have thought?"

The voice was still gentle and soft. "That's part

14

of the price, Benny. Are you willing to pay the price for the anointing?"

I Had Been Told Before

Yes, there *is* power in the presence of the Holy Spirit that I wrote about in *Good Morning, Holy Spirit*. And there *is* the power of the anointing that I want to teach you about in this book. And there *is* a price we each must pay for it. This Detroit episode, once again, drove home all three facts. The presence of the Holy Spirit leads us to live in the power of the anointing if we are willing to pay the price of obedience.

Kathryn Kuhlman, who was so important in my introduction to the Holy Spirit and to the truths of both the presence and the anointing of the Spirit, had talked about "the price." She had paid it.

I have also never forgotten my encounters with a man in England who had a tremendous anointing of the Spirit upon his life. Every time I got near him, my legs would shake. Sometimes I would feel weak by just looking at him.

One day I prayed, "Lord, let Your anointing be on me as it is on him."

The Lord spoke back to me: "Pay the price, and I will give it to you."

"What is the price?" I asked.

The answer didn't come immediately. But one day it came suddenly from the Holy Spirit. He showed it to me in Acts 4:13: "Now when they saw the boldness of Peter and John, and perceived that they were uneducated and untrained men, they marveled. *And they realized that they had been with Jesus.*"

That is the key — to be with Jesus — over and over and over, constantly, not just a few minutes a day, not just occasionally. In Detroit I had been with Jesus on Saturday night. But I had refused to be alone with Him later when He beckoned.

The presence and the anointing. As you read on, you will learn how the Holy Spirit can lead you to experience the fullness and the power of the Godhead each and every day. Once you grasp what the anointing holds for you, experiencing the depth and rich reality of that precious touch, you will never be the same.

Chapter 2

The Most Valuable Gift

What do you value most as a Christian?"

People have asked me that for years. And each time my answer is the same. Except for my salvation, I value the anointing the most.

The phrase *the anointing* may be unfamiliar to some of you. This book should change that.

As I wrote in my previous volume, *Good Morning, Holy Spirit*, I have never been the same since God first graced my life with the precious anointing of His Holy Spirit. And those last four words are important. The anointing is the anointing *of the Holy Spirit,* and it is performed by the Lord Jesus Christ. No human can do it.

Having had that glorious encounter, which I will discuss in the next chapter, I would rather die than live one day without it. That sounds dramatic in our age of "selfism" and humanism, but it is the truth. My constant prayer is simply this, and I believe it will become yours: "God, please don't ever take Your anointing from me. I would rather die than face a future without Your touch on my life. May I never know a day without the anointing of Your Holy Spirit."

What God has taught me about that special touch of the anointing has caused me to treasure my relationship with our ever-present Companion, the Holy Spirit, even more. I know now that there are several types of anointing, and I will explore that in later chapters. And I know that it is possible for me to forsake the Master and forfeit this intimate relationship that I value with my entire being. I could, by an act of the will, turn my back on Him and alienate myself from fellowship. But I will never do that. As I've said before, I'd rather die than lose His touch.

My goal is to deepen my relationship with God and to grow to a greater dimension of the anointing. For, despite the unbelievable experiences He has given me, I know He has more ahead for His children. I want to share this incredible adventure with you.

Dear friend, I want you to know God has a special touch for your life today. "This is your day," as we proclaim on my daily television program. It can be today and every day of your life if you desire, a day of the reality of the Holy Spirit with you — the anointing.

Your Desire Can Be Fulfilled

Perhaps you are like so many who have said, "Benny, I desire to experience God's power in my life, but I really don't know how to make that happen. I love God, and I know that He loves me. But I have a longing for a deeper, more intimate relationship. I don't want to know *about* Him; I want to *know* Him and to experience the reality of His power regularly."

Be assured that your desire can be fulfilled. He's heard you cry. The first thing He would have you know is that He intensely desires His children — all of them — to experience His presence, not once or twice, but every day. He longs for them to know not only His presence, but also His communion and power.

Nevertheless, my friend, you cannot know the power of God's anointing until you experience the presence of God. Many have misunderstood the real meaning and essence of "the anointing." They think it is some "goosebump" experience that is only a matter of feelings and thus short-lived. That is untrue. When the anointing of the Spirit comes upon your life, all confusion will vanish. You will be transformed forever.

I can remember the first time I felt that sweet, awesome, powerful, rushing river of the anointing coursing through me. It was as though I was wrapped in a blanket of His love. It was unmistakable. The warmth of His presence surrounded me. My surroundings faded into the shadows as I basked in the presence of the Holy Spirit. There was no mistaking who He was. I was overwhelmed by love and His closeness. I felt total peace, and yet I exploded with ecstasy.

You, too, can know God this intimately as you experience the anointing and power of His Spirit — today, tomorrow, and always.

Are You Dead to Self?

Only when you abandon self, totally emptying yourself, can you be filled with God's presence. Then, and only then, can you see Acts 1:8 — the promise of power, which I will discuss later — fulfilled in your life. For as His presence envelops you, His power can begin to pour out of you.

In this book, I will tell you about the death to self, which sounds so frightening and impossible. And I will share how I first came to experience the anointing and how that moment revolutionized my life. As I wrote in *Good Morning, Holy Spirit*, things changed — radically. My relationship with God's Spirit has deepened steadily since that first day. He is a part of my daily and hourly existence. I never begin a morning without inviting Him to come and enable me to walk with Him throughout the day.

It is important also that you understand the Spirit is vitally interested in every aspect of your life. He doesn't divide things up into spiritual and secular. There is no secular. He wants to be — and actually is — involved in everything.

In the first part of the book, I will tell you about this person called the Holy Spirit. So many know so little of Him, and *He is God*. They ignore Him, never talking to Him, never asking Him to be a daily, minute-by-minute part of their existence. They seem to prefer pleading and begging, then becoming irritated when they see no answers.

How wrong this is. The Bible says, "Draw near to God and He will draw near to you" (James 4:8). It's time to do that. It's time to say, "Here I am, Holy Spirit. Come. Walk with me. Help me receive what the Father has for me. Help me hear what the Lord is saying."

When I say, "Come, Holy Spirit," the chaos and confusion of life in the world cease. Darkness turns to light. My empty heart is filled, and my ears are opened to hear the voice of the Father. For the voice of God is absent without the presence of the Holy Spirit surrounding you.

You may ask, "Why doesn't the Holy Spirit, if He's God and knows everything, just help us and give us what we need?"

The answer is that He is a gentleman and will never push His way into your life. But the second you say, "Holy Spirit, help me receive what I'm asking for," He comes and helps you receive through Jesus what you have asked the Father for. You see, He wants communion and fellowship with you. He's seeking a moment-by-moment relationship, one in which you can actually have the mind of Christ (1 Cor. 2:16).

When the Holy Spirit is a reality in your life, He provides an avenue through which the anointing, the power, can flow.

Do you remember when Peter, James, and John were with the Lord on the Mount of Transfiguration (Matt. 17:1ff)? The cloud settled on them. What is the cloud? It is the Holy Spirit. When you read in the Old Testament of the cloud descending upon the Tabernacle (Exod. 40:34), you are reading of the Holy Spirit.

Also, when Jesus ascended after His resurrection, a cloud received Him (Acts 1 :9). Again, that was the Holy Spirit. Similarly, when Jesus returns, He will be riding on the same cloud (Acts 1:11).

In these cases, when the Lord spoke, where was the voice? It was in the cloud. The Holy Spirit is the one who brings the voice of God into your heart with clarity.

If you haven't experienced a daily walk in which these things are reality, you need to understand what the presence and the anointing are. I do not want to limit God and what He will do in your life, but I know that, as you receive the Spirit's presence, seven things found in the beautiful eighth chapter of the book of Romans will occur in your life. By themselves they are worth everything:

- You will be liberated from sin. You, like so many others, may have struggled in an area of your life that you have not been able to overcome for years. The Bible says you will not be liberated from the law of sin until you follow the Spirit.
- Righteousness will enter your life naturally, as you learn to "walk after the Spirit." You won't force it in. Your struggle for righteous-

ness will give way to its abiding, easy flow.

- Your mentality will be changed. You will be freed from setting your mind "on the things of the flesh" to set them "on the things of the Spirit."
- You will become totally at peace. For Paul says that "to be spiritually minded is peace."
- You will be healed from your head to your toes. For "He who raised Christ from the dead will give life to [quicken] your mortal bodies," which the great majority of the Body of Christ badly needs.
- You will receive the total death to self and total life to God. For Paul says that "if you by the Spirit put to death the deeds of the body, you will live."
- You will receive intimacy with the Father, as by the Spirit you look up into His face and say, "Abba, Father — Daddy."

On top of all of that, you will receive power to serve the Almighty, which I know, by having met so many of you personally at miracle crusades around the country, you are hungering for — ready to pay that price mentioned in the first chapter.

I am excited to be able to share these experiences and these understandings with you. For I know that the presence of the Holy Spirit and His anointing, multiplied among the millions of God's people, are the way the Lord will reach the needy world in our time. I pray that you are as excited about this as I am.

Chapter 3

In the Beginning

Sitting on the floor of my bedroom that December night in 1973, I wrestled with the words I had heard a few hours earlier. Mysterious words. Strong words. Why had I not heard them before?

I should have been tired, for it was after eleven o'clock; I had been up since well before dawn. But my mind would not stop racing over the events of that life-shaking day.

A friend had taken me to a meeting in Pittsburgh led by a healing evangelist of whom I knew very little. Her name was Kathryn Kuhlman. I saw, heard, and experienced things in Pittsburgh that would alter the course of my life forever.

I had been saved for a year or two, having recently been introduced to the charismatic movement by some school friends. I knew almost nothing about the Spirit-led life. I was starving; I was desperate. But I found little to nourish my soul. Now this. What had she meant that day?

Once again, I thought back over the Kuhlman

meeting. Her message had been titled "The Secret Power of the Holy Spirit." I remembered my first impression of this unusual lady in her flowing white dress, almost dancing across the platform, floating as if plugged into some invisible power. I also remembered the rather embarrassing vibrating and shaking I had undergone for two hours before and even an hour during the meeting, only to enter into the most rapturous worship I had ever dreamed possible. I knew beyond doubt in those hours that the Lord was right there. His presence was certain.

My prayer life to that point had been that of the average, serious-minded Christian. But in those few hours in Pittsburgh, I was not just talking to the Lord; He was talking to me. He was showing me His love; He was convincing me of His mercy and kindness. And what a communion that was!

Later on, I looked up from my deep fellowship to see Miss Kuhlman sobbing, her face buried in her hands. She sobbed terribly, and before long, everything was quiet. The music stopped; the ushers froze. This went on for several minutes. Stone silence.

Then, in a flash, she threw her head back, and her eyes were flashing, aflame. Aflame! I had never seen anything like it. Boldness rang out from her entire being. Then, like an arrow, her long finger was thrust forward. Power seemed to shoot from it. But there was more — yes, pain and emotion, all shooting from that bony finger.

She sobbed again momentarily and then spoke,

which doesn't really describe the agony and drama in her voice, but there is no adequate word beyond *spoke*.

"Please," she pleaded. The word was stretched to its limit. "Pleeeaaassse . . . don't grieve the Holy Spirit." She said it again, "Please don't grieve the Holy Spirit."

No one moved. Certainly not I, although I felt her finger was pointing right at me, which made me nervous. And I'm sure others felt the same way.

Then, her voice touched with a sob, she went on, "Don't you understand?" The words hung in the air. "He's all I've got!"

I didn't know what she was talking about, but I soaked everything in.

She wasn't finished: "Please! Don't wound Him. He's all I've got. Don't wound the one I love!"

Moments later, she stuck her long bony finger out again — I know it was pointed right at me — and said, "He's more real than anything in this world! He's more real than you are!"

I lay out this scene for you again to drive home one of the most important points we Christians must grasp, especially as we move toward a realization of the presence and the anointing of the Holy Spirit. Kathryn Kuhlman was talking about a person, a person more real than you or I — a person, not an "it," not a mist, not a force, not some spooky, eerie, floating substance accompanied by pipe organs and harps. The Holy Spirit is a person with a personality, a nature. And He is God — an equal member of the three-person Godhead, containing the whole nature of the God-head, the one undivided God, at work in creation, redemption, and empowerment. You must never forget that truth.

All I knew that December night back in my Toronto room was that I wanted what Kathryn Kuhlman had. Whatever she meant when she said, "He's all I have" — that is what I wanted.

And There He Was

Sometime that night, I felt compelled to pray, as though someone were pulling me to my knees. And the first words out of my mouth were "Holy Spirit." I had never done that before. It's hard to realize now, but you must remember that I had never even considered that the Holy Spirit was a person to be addressed. I had talked only to the Father and to the Son.

I mustered my courage and said, "Holy Spirit, Kathryn says You are her Friend. I don't think I know You. Before today, I thought I did. But after that meeting, I realize I really don't. I don't think I know You. Can I meet You? Can I really meet You?"

Nothing seemed to happen. But as I questioned and doubted myself, eyes closed, something like electricity shot through me and I began to vibrate all over, just as I had in Pittsburgh. The only difference was that I was sitting in my pajamas on my bedroom floor in my parents' home in Toronto.

27

And it was very late at night. But I was tingling with the power of God's Spirit. He was present in my room! My life would never be the same.

And neither will yours, my friend, if you will act upon what I say here.

A Year-long Lesson

My introduction had been so real that when I woke very early the next morning, I did what seemed to be the most natural thing in the world. I said, "Good Morning, Holy Spirit," and I still say it every morning. He is present and yearns to participate in our lives from our first waking moment each day.

That first morning, the glorious atmosphere of the previous night unmistakably returned, but there was no shaking or vibrating. I was simply wrapped in His presence.

That began a year of intense experience with the sweet presence of the Spirit, a year of fellowship and communion, of Spirit-led study of the Bible, of listening to the one described in God's Word as Teacher, Counselor, Comforter.

I told in my previous book about the problems with my family after my conversion to Jesus Christ. Having been born into a Greek family in Israel, where my father was the mayor of Jaffa, and having been educated in Roman Catholic schools, I was thoroughly ostracized by my family after I had publicly accepted the Lord Jesus. It became so bad that my father would not even speak to me, and other relatives scorned or ignored me.

This was compounded by my inability to talk fluently because of a severe stutter. This meant that I spent hours alone in my room. But after my introduction to the Holy Spirit, this worked for good, allowing me to delight in the incalculable richness of His presence.

Before long, I became like Miss Kuhlman in valuing that presence above everything else in life. I am talking about a realization that exceeds the baptism in the Holy Spirit, speaking in tongues, and other aspects of normal charismatic Christian life as I had experienced it. Yes, I did speak in tongues, and I did attend a charismatic church faithfully. But there was more to this experience than that.

The Holy Spirit became real to me. He became my Companion. When I opened the Bible, I knew He was there with me as though He were sitting beside me. He patiently taught me and loved me. I didn't see His face, of course, but I knew where He was. And I began to know His personality.

Jesus had said He would not leave His disciples — you and me — helpless but would send one to be with us and to lead us. And now I knew firsthand that He had kept His word.

The Purpose Is Revealed

It's important that I repeat an episode from *Good Morning, Holy Spirit* to place these remarkable experiences in perspective and to show that the Christian life is not intended to be a "bless-me, gimme" club.

After numerous inquiries to the Lord as to why He was allowing me to experience the reality of His presence, I had a frightening vision. I saw someone standing in front of me, engulfed in flames and moving uncontrollably. His feet were not touching the ground. His mouth was opening and closing, like the "gnashing of teeth" in the Bible.

At that moment, the Lord spoke in an audible voice: "Preach the gospel."

I responded: "But, Lord, I can't talk."

Two nights later, I had a dream. I saw an angel with a chain in his hand; it was attached to a door that seemed to fill heaven. He pulled it open, and there were people as far as the eye could see. They were all moving toward a large, deep valley, and that valley was an inferno. Thousands were falling into the fire. Those on the front lines were trying to fight it, but the crush of humanity pushed them into the flames.

Again the Lord spoke to me: "If you do not preach, I will hold you responsible."

I knew instantly that everything in my life, including my unbelievable experiences in recent months, was for one purpose: to move me to preach the gospel.

A Spectacular Change

In early December 1974, I visited Stan and Shirley Phillips in Oshawa, about thirty miles east of Toronto, and I still hadn't obeyed the vision to preach. Indeed, I hadn't told anyone about my experiences, dreams, and visions. But that was to change.

"Can I tell you something?" I asked. They both nodded expectantly and I poured out my heart to them, at least to the extent my stutter would allow. They were very patient and listened for about three hours.

Finally Stan interrupted me and said enthusiastically, "Benny, tonight you must come to our church and share this."

Stan and Shirley were part of a group of about a hundred people called Shiloh, at the Trinity Assembly of God in Oshawa, so I went with them that evening — long hair, casual clothes, stuttering tongue, and all. I didn't know what would happen. I knew I had been told to preach the gospel, but I had come to think that the preaching would probably be through tracts.

I still didn't know what was going to happen as I sat in the audience during the early part of the service. I became very nervous — scared. I was going to make a fool of myself, and everyone would laugh. I didn't need any more of that.

31

Before long, Stan, a scientist at a nuclear plant in the area, had introduced me and I was walking to the pulpit. I had never stood behind one.

Stan had said, "Share your experiences," and that's what I set out to do. I opened my mouth, terrified, and something touched my tongue, numbing it. I talked, fluently and rapidly, actually too rapidly; I had to tell myself to slow down.

I was preaching the gospel! It seemed impossible, but I was talking clearly and smoothly. And I haven't stopped.

I told them — they were mostly young people — about meeting the Holy Spirit in my room and then talking to Him, asking Him questions, and listening to Him for a year.

"How do you meet the Holy Ghost?" I asked rhetorically. "On your knees, lying on your back, walking around the room, praying. You don't meet Him by just singing a song."

I pressed ahead: "There's only one way to the Father, Son, and Holy Spirit, and that's through prayer."

I kept up that kind of talk for about an hour, and then realized I should be drawing to a close. But I wanted to tell them about Moses, for the Holy Spirit had given me insight that still amazes me. And I was getting bold all of a sudden.

"Moses asked the Lord — now nobody can ask this until he's in the Holy of Holies," I said. "It was a time, forty days later, before he could ask — remember, God had touched him, fellowship had erupted, worship, beauty, ecstasy, the presence of the Almighty, boldness had set in. Then he could say, 'Let me see Your glory.'

"He had paid the price," I said. "He was saying, 'Lord, I've been up here with you for the last forty days. There's nothing left of my flesh. Let me see Your glory.' And God passed before him. And although he saw only His back, he saw the glory, the wonder of God."

I didn't let up. "Do you want God's presence?" I asked. "Then lose your own. You lose sight of yourself, and you'll gain sight of God."

I wound down and I thought, "I'm going to pray." In my room, I had always wobbled and even fallen when I invited the Holy Spirit in, so much so that I looked for a safe place to stand or kneel, even putting my back to the wall. But I didn't have any expectation that something similar would happen in an open meeting.

So I lifted my hands and said, "Holy Spirit, you are welcome here. Please come."

Instantly the power of God hit the place. People began to cry and many fell to the floor.

"Oh, dear God, what do I do now?" I asked.

I turned around to the fellow who was leading the meeting, hoping he would come and take the service out of my hands. But as I turned and pointed toward him, he fell backward several feet. I was trying to get him to come close and suddenly he was farther away. No one could get near me. And then I realized that during all those times over the past year, anyone who might have been in the room would have fallen under the power too.

The leader made several tries at getting close to me, and each time he hit the wall.

Finally I just talked to the people. Many were on their knees, still weeping. I told them more about the person of the Holy Spirit. Finally I ended without praying any more.

Isaiah 10:27 says that "the yoke shall be destroyed because of the anointing" (KJV) and that is exactly what happened. The devil's hold on lives is destroyed when the anointing comes. That was the case with me and my tongue, and that was true of the people in the congregation.

As I realized more fully later, "religious" activity, loud tongues, moans, and groans are not necessary prerequisites for the power of God to be revealed. More often than not, they are a hindrance because they can come from the flesh, and God wants to demonstrate real power. Our greatest desire should not be for spiritual gifts, but for the presence and the power of God. Gifts may not change your life, but the presence and power will. And that was what I was tasting for the first time that night in Oshawa.

As I've said hundreds of times over the years, God is never late. He is never too early, but He is never too late either. When the numbing hit, I simply said, "That's it!" and charged ahead. The anointing of the Holy Spirit had come, I had been healed, and my preaching took on power.

Miraculously my ministry began and instantly

mushroomed. Virtually every day, invitations came from churches and fellowships to minister.

It's important to note that I had experienced the presence of the Holy Spirit a year earlier, and that He had taught me meticulously and lovingly, assuring me, encouraging me, loving me for a whole year. I had obeyed Him to the fullest extent of my understanding, and the anointing had come, just as it will to you. It is for everyone. Once you grasp what the anointing holds for you, experiencing the depth and rich reality of that precious touch, life will take on new meaning as you move into the place of service that the Lord has for you.

A Strong Warning

I will never forget going home from Oshawa that night. I was stunned. As I lay on my bed an hour later, I was still numb and puzzled by the events of the evening. I had seen the true power of God. I had caught a glimpse, but only a fleeting one — of the answer to Kathryn Kuhlman's statement: "If you find the power — if you find the power — you will find heaven's treasure." It was only a hint, and I needed to understand more. I was so inexperienced.

"What did you do tonight, Lord?" I asked into the darkness.

Unexpectedly I heard a quick answer: "Be faithful." That was all. "Be faithful."

The next morning I turned on the radio shortly after waking, following my habit of listening to church services as I got ready to go to church myself. The first thing I heard — and I don't have any clue as to the speaker — was: "Watch what you do with the power you have." Then the program instantly went off the air. I can't explain it. I had turned on the radio, a voice had said, "Watch what you do with the power you have," and the voice was gone. I couldn't find it again as I fiddled with the dials.

Of course, I realize now that the words *be faithful* from the previous night and the strong warning on the radio the next morning went together. They said, in essence, "Be careful with the power I've given you. Don't play games. And don't misuse it."

That is a warning for all who seek and receive the anointing of the Spirit. God must be able to trust you.

He longs for us to know and experience His presence and His anointing. When we are emptied of self, we will know His presence. Only then can we experience His power — the anointing of the Holy Spirit. But the trust factor is also very important. We must be faithful with what God so richly supplies.

Chapter 4

An Answer at Last

When I look back over my life and see all the ways it could have been so different, I marvel at God's grace and mercy.

Think of it. I was born into a very traditional Middle Eastern family with a strong emphasis on discipline and tradition, having no relationship with a personal God. I was born and raised a Greek in Israel and educated in Roman Catholic schools by nuns. I was stricken in early childhood by a severe stutter that made oral communication unbelievably difficult, almost impossible. I was uprooted at age fifteen when my family moved to Toronto. I was forced to learn a fourth language, English, behind Arabic, Hebrew, and French, which I had previously spoken in Catholic schools. I was taken from the cloistered confines of a Catholic school to the public schools of Toronto. I was a loner — quiet, shy, and uncertain.

Guidelines and Traditions

The Lord wondrously saved me through some fellow students when I was nineteen, although I had had glorious encounters with Him before, such as in dreams and visions.

Prior to my rebirth, I had tried to conform to all the directives and guidelines prescribed by those in authority over me. I had observed all the traditions tied to my Catholic education and honestly attempted to obey those I viewed as God's representatives in my life. I was a good student and did as I was instructed by the nuns (making the sign of the cross when passing a Catholic church, maintaining regular prayer, and the like). I'm sure I considered myself to be a Christian, but I did not feel complete or fulfilled.

Immediately after my salvation experience, I began attending a church of three thousand young people in downtown Toronto. I was not accustomed to that kind of charismatic meeting, with its spontaneous, unpredictable responses at various volume levels. I was more attuned to reserved, deliberate, and predictable activity.

These were a different kind of people. They hugged one another and joy seemed to radiate from their faces. Of course, at that time I knew nothing about the charismatic movement. I only knew that I was in unfamiliar surroundings.

Partly because of my mistaken evaluation of spirituality, my most serious reaction came some time later, after I had been baptized in the Holy Spirit. I found myself watching one man in particular, whom I thought to be the most spiritual person in the church. I watched him lift his hands upward; he had them up almost constantly. His body shook a little. His lips would quiver while his eyes looked toward heaven. And when he prayed in this unfamiliar language — tongues — he would always say the same thing, as though repeating something over and over. Every time I heard him pray, it was the same. He shook, and he said the same thing.

Naive and hungry for the things of God, I went to him one day and asked if I could talk to him. He seemed friendly enough.

"I am so hungry for more," I said. "How do I find what I am looking for?"

He looked at me and asked, "Have you been baptized in the Holy Spirit?"

"Yes," I answered, eager to receive guidance.

"Do you speak in other tongues?" he asked.

"Yes," I replied.

He looked at me and said matter-of-factly, "What more do you want?"

I was stunned and, after a discreet moment, walked away in silence. *What more do I want,* I thought. *If this is all there is, I'm not sure there's much to it.*

I desperately wanted more of God, certain in my soul that there was more. The pages of the Bible said so, but I didn't know what to do. I didn't know what God was offering or how to get it. No one seemed able to help me.

I switched churches in 1973 and met a wonderful man, Jim Poynter, a Free Methodist minister, who became a dear friend and one day introduced me to the Kathryn Kuhlman ministry. That set in motion the events I described in the previous chapters. Otherwise I would not have learned of the wonderful presence of God and the anointing of the Holy Spirit, both of which are for every believer.

The Lord wants to give us so much more than many of us have believed possible. I want to share with you the ways the Lord taught me since that amazing day when He loosed my tongue and began to empower me for ministry. These wonderful possibilities are for you also, and I pray that God will inspire you and lead you forward so that together we will fulfill His plan for the extraordinary time in which we live.

The Way It Started

Before I share the ways in which the Lord taught and empowered me for ministry, I want to take you back and give you more insight into that glorious day in Pittsburgh when I met the Holy Spirit at a Kathryn Kuhlman meeting.

That day of December 21, 1973, began at five o'clock in the morning after my new friend Jim Poynter and I had ridden with a large group in a charter bus from Toronto to Pittsburgh through a terrible snowstorm. We had fallen into our hotel beds only four hours earlier.

Jim insisted that we get to the First Presbyterian Church in downtown Pittsburgh by six o'clock or we wouldn't get a seat, so it was pitch dark when we arrived. Even then, hundreds of people were already there, and the doors weren't supposed to open for two hours. It was freezing cold, and I was wearing everything I had with me — boots, gloves, the works.

Being small has some advantages. I began inching my way closer and closer to the doors, pulling Jim behind me. I couldn't believe the crowd! "It's like this every week," a woman said.

As I stood there, I suddenly began to vibrate — as if someone had gripped my body and begun to shake it. I thought for a moment that the bitter air had gotten to me. But I was dressed warmly, and I certainly didn't feel cold. An uncontrollable shaking had just come over me. Nothing like that had happened before. And it didn't stop. I was too embarrassed to tell Jim, but I could feel my very bones rattling. I felt it in my knees. In my mouth. *What's happening to me?* I wondered. *Is this the power of God?* I didn't understand.

A Race for the Front

By this time the doors were about to open, and the crowd pressed forward until I could barely move. Still the vibrating didn't stop.

Jim said, "Benny, when those doors open, run just as fast as you can."

"Why?" I asked.

41

"If you don't, they'll run right over you." He'd been there before.

I had never thought I'd be in a race going to church, but there I was. And when the doors opened, I took off like an Olympic sprinter. I passed everybody: old women, young men, all of them. In fact, I made it right to the front row and tried to sit down. An usher told me the first row was reserved. I learned later that Miss Kuhlman's staff handpicked the people who sat in the front row. She was so sensitive to the Spirit that she wanted only positive, praying supporters right in front of her.

With my severe stuttering problem, I knew it would be useless to argue with the usher. The second row was already filled, but Jim and I found a spot in row three.

It would be another hour before the service began, so I took off my coat, gloves, and boots. As I relaxed, I realized I was shaking more than before. It just wouldn't stop. The vibrations were going through my arms and legs as if I were attached to some kind of machine. The experience was foreign to me. To be honest, I was scared.

As the organ played, all I could think about was the shaking. It wasn't a "sick" feeling. It wasn't as if I were catching a cold or a virus. In fact, the longer it continued, the more beautiful it became. It was an unusual sensation that didn't really seem physical at all.

At that moment, almost out of nowhere, Kathryn Kuhlman appeared. In an instant, the atmo-

42

sphere in the building was charged. I didn't know what to expect. I didn't feel anything around me. No voices. No heavenly angels singing. Nothing. All I knew was that I had been shaking for three hours.

Then, as the singing began, I found myself doing something I had never expected. I was on my feet. My hands were lifted, and tears streamed down my face as we sang "How Great Thou Art."

It was as if I had exploded. Never before had tears gushed from my eyes so quickly. Talk about ecstasy! It was a feeling of intense glory.

I wasn't singing the way I normally sang in church. I sang with my entire being. And when we came to the words, "Then sings my soul, my Savior God, to thee," I literally sang it from my soul.

I was so lost in the Spirit of that song that it took a few moments for me to realize my shaking had stopped.

But the atmosphere of the service continued. I thought I had been raptured. I was worshiping beyond anything I had experienced. It was like coming face to face with pure spiritual truth. Whether anyone else felt it or not, I did.

In my young Christian experience, God had touched my life, but never as He was touching me that day.

Like a Wave

As I stood there, continuing to worship the Lord, I opened my eyes to look around because I suddenly felt a draft. I didn't know where it was coming from. It was gentle and slow, like a breeze.

I looked at the stained-glass windows. But they were all closed. And they were much too high to allow such a draft.

The unusual breeze I felt, however, was more like a wave. I felt it go down one arm and up the other. I actually felt it moving.

What was happening? Could I ever have the courage to tell anyone what I felt? They would think I'd lost my mind.

For what seemed like ten minutes, the waves of that wind continued to wash over me. And then I felt as if someone had wrapped my body in a pure blanket — a blanket of warmth.

Kathryn began to minister to the people, but I was so lost in the Spirit that it really didn't matter to me. The Lord was closer to me than ever before.

I felt I needed to talk to the Lord, but all I could whisper was, "Dear Jesus, please have mercy on me." I said it again, "Jesus, please have mercy on me."

I felt so unworthy. I felt like Isaiah when he entered the presence of the Lord.

Woe is me, for I am undone!
Because I am a man of unclean lips,
And I dwell in the midst of a people of
  unclean lips;
For my eyes have seen the King,
The LORD of hosts. (Isa. 6:5)

The same thing happened when people saw Christ. They immediately saw their own filth, their need of cleansing.

That is what happened to me. It was as if a giant spotlight was beaming down on me. All I could see were my weaknesses, my faults, and my sins.

Again and again I said, "Dear Jesus, please have mercy on me."

Then I heard a voice that I knew must be the Lord's. It was ever so gentle, but it was unmistakable. He said to me, "My mercy is abundant on you."

My prayer life to that point was that of a normal, average Christian. But at that moment in the service I was not just talking to the Lord. He was talking to me. And, oh, what a communion that was!

Little did I realize that what was happening to me in the third row of the First Presbyterian Church in Pittsburgh was just a foretaste of what God had planned for the future.

Those words rang in my ears: "My mercy is abundant on you."

I sat down crying and sobbing. There was just

nothing in my life to compare with what I felt. I was so filled and transformed by the Spirit that nothing else mattered. I didn't care if a nuclear bomb hit Pittsburgh and the whole world blew up. At that moment I felt, as the Word describes it, "Peace . . . which surpasses all understanding" (Phil. 4:7).

Jim had told me about the miracles that took place in Miss Kuhlman's meetings. But I had no idea what I was about to witness in the next three hours. People who were deaf suddenly could hear. A woman got up out of her wheelchair. There were testimonies of healings for tumors, arthritis, headaches, and more. Even her severest critics have acknowledged the genuine healings that took place in her meetings.

The service was long, but it seemed like a fleeting moment. Never in my life had I been so moved and touched by God's power.

A Later Meeting

Shortly after that amazing encounter with the Holy Spirit, I returned to another Kuhlman meeting in which she spoke of the price she had paid for the anointing on her ministry and the secret to the power of the Holy Spirit. She talked about death to self, carrying the cross, paying the price. She often said things such as: "Any of you ministers can have what I have if you'll only pay the price."

In that service I began to understand that there is a higher experience, something more than just the presence of the Holy Spirit. There is an anointing, an empowering for service, and that comes through paying the price.

Understanding the Price

What is the price? It has taken me many years to reach this understanding, and I want to share it with you.

In Psalm 63 David says,

O GOD, You are my God;
Early will I seek You;
My soul thirsts for You;
My flesh longs for You
In a dry and thirsty land
Where there is no water.
So I have looked for You in the
   sanctuary,
To see Your Power and Your glory.

He had seen a glimpse of God's power and glory. He was longing for it. But how was he to get it?

Here the Holy Spirit began to open my eyes and make me understand what Miss Kuhlman meant when she spoke about the price and about dying.

David declares that his flesh "longs" for God, while his soul "thirsts." Isaiah, meanwhile, in 26:9, says that with his spirit he will "seek" God. So we have the flesh longing for God, the soul thirsting, and the spirit seeking. It is noteworthy that in Moses' accounts of the Tabernacle we find: the Outer Court, which is symbolic of the flesh; the Holy Place, which is symbolic of the soul; and the Holy of Holies, which is symbolic of the spirit. Longing takes one to the Outer Court; thirsting takes one to the Holy Place; and seeking leads one to the Holy of Holies.

So as we long for God we go into prayer, which is the place where God begins to deal with and crucify the flesh. It is a place of struggle where, as we get on our knees each day, all we can think about at first is our guilt, our failures, our great needs. We repeat ourselves over and over, and God seems a million miles away. We wonder if we're accomplishing anything. We want to fall asleep, to take a break — anything.

What we don't immediately realize is that the longer we are on our knees, the less of the flesh remains. A death begins as we are on our knees.

Soon, as God finishes crucifying the flesh, a breakthrough comes — you feel it — and suddenly your prayer becomes real. A river gushes out of your inmost being, and your words become meaningful. The presence of God comes in, and something real happens to you. You may even begin to weep.

That breakthrough may take a half hour, an hour, maybe longer. It will take as long as needed, depending on where you are with the Lord, what your relationship is with Him. He must deal with the idols and the sins in your heart. Any Isaacs in your heart must die (which is what God was determining with Abraham). If you haven't prayed for a long time, you can't expect a breakthrough after the first minute or two.

Remember, this is a daily matter. The breakthrough doesn't come once for all time. "I die daily," Paul says in 1 Corinthians 15:31. There will be a struggle each time we go into this kind of prayer. The presence and the anointing don't come today because you died twenty years ago. They come today because you died this morning. God does not use leftovers.

The way you will know when the breakthrough comes is that guilt will disappear. The absence of guilt means you have broken through. You have sought Him and found Him.

At some point, then, will come the "thirsting" for Him. Your soul will thirst for God. David said in Psalm 42:1-2,

As the deer pants for the water brooks,
So pants my soul for You, O God.
My soul thirsts for God, for the living God.
When shall I come and appear before God?

And that is exactly what happens to us. Our soul thirsts to come before the living God; it thirsts for His presence.

David's imagery is perfect. A deer seeks water for two reasons; one, because he is thirsty and, two, because he is being chased by another animal. He knows that his scent will be lost if he gets into the water. He will be safe. So it is with us believers. We thirst for the presence of God because it satisfies our souls and because no enemy can touch us. The devil cannot find us. That's why David also wrote, "You are my hiding place" (Ps. 32:7).

So when you find that water for which your soul has been longing, praise will erupt in you. You will know that you are in the Holy Place, where praise is genuine. There will be none of the matter-of-fact and routine "praise the Lord; thank you, Lord." It will become *real*. Every part of your being will be thanking Him — even for those things that an hour ago you could not thank Him for. Everything will become beautiful.

Now the Holy of Holies

Do you remember that in Psalm 63:2, David spoke of wanting to see God's "power and glory"? That comes with the third stage of the price, the seeking and dying to self that must come before the anointing. This is found in the Holy of Holies, symbolic of the spirit. It is the place where you say nothing, you do nothing. You don't pray. You don't sing. You receive.

That's the place David meant when he said in Psalm 42:7,

Deep calls unto deep at the noise of Your
   waterfalls;
all Your waves and billows have gone over
   me.

In the Outer Court, my mouth was talking to God. In the Holy Place, my soul was talking. In the Holy of Holies, my spirit talks — deep calling unto deep. This is where prayer without ceasing is born — where you bask in the glory of God. You are not longing. You are not thirsting. You are drinking.

"Be still, and know that I am God," David wrote in Psalm 46:10. You are so full that you cannot talk. Words are inadequate. You are totally in His presence. You are not interested in what He can do for you; you are interested in knowing Him.

Those who experience this are the ones God can trust with the anointing, as you will see later. God will not trust the anointing to those who don't love Him, who do not put Him as number one.

Let me assure you that, as you enter the Holy of Holies on a daily basis, it becomes more natural, quicker. It may not take you a half hour to break through; it may take five minutes. I have had times when the second I said, "Lord," there it was. Also, the more time you remain in the presence of God, the more that presence will rub off on you. The thicker it will get, you might say.

For example, the first time you break through, you might come out of your room and say to your wife, "Hello, darling," and she will know as you talk that you have been in the presence of God. A week later, say, as you have been spending more and more time with the Lord, you will walk out and before you say anything, she will feel the glory. You won't have to say anything.

With Peter the apostle this reached the point where people expected to be healed when his shadow fell upon them (Acts 5:15).

Putting on Strength

Pursuing this theme, we should now look at Isaiah 52:1-2:

> Awake, awake!
> Put on your strength, O Zion;
> Put on your beautiful garments,
> O Jerusalem, the holy city!
> For the uncircumcised and the unclean
> Shall no longer come to you.
> Shake yourself from the dust, arise,
> And sit down, O Jerusalem;
> Loose yourself from the bonds of your
>   neck,
> O captive daughter of Zion!

"Awaking" in Scripture has to do with prayer. When it says, "Awake, awake," it means, "Pray, pray." You will recall that the Lord Jesus, finding the apostles sleeping as He awaited His betrayer in Gethsemane, said, "Watch and pray" (Matt. 26:41), or "Stay awake and pray; be alert."

It's a command; we must pray. Jeremiah 10:25 shows us that God will judge the prayerless — "the families who do not call on Your name" —

52

with the world. We are commanded to seek the Lord.

So the passage begins by telling us to awake, awake, shake ourselves out of lethargy, pay the price, seek the Lord with all our might, enter into deep prayer, deep love, make Him our number one priority. Then six things will occur:

(1) We will put on spiritual strength — strength against Satan, strength against sin, strength against temptation. Weakness will go.
(2) We will put on new holy garments, the garments of righteousness. Sin will not be able to touch us.
(3) The uncircumcized and unclean will not be a part of us. We will no longer have fellowship with the wicked.
(4) We will stop running here and there looking for someone to pray for us or get us out of trouble. We will shake ourselves from the dust — from our misery, from our mess. We will arise and be free.
(5) And then we can sit down and rest. There will be peace — real peace, the peace of Jesus.
(6) We will loose ourselves from the grip of Satan and the sin that keeps coming back upon us.

The Other Side of the Coin

If we read on into Isaiah 52:3-5, we find the results of not awaking or of remaining prayerless. This surely will shake everyone of us awake:

For thus says the LORD:
"You have sold yourselves for nothing,
And you shall be redeemed without
money."
For thus says the LORD GOD:
"My people went down at first
Into Egypt to sojourn there;
Then the Assyrian oppressed them without
cause.
Now therefore, what have I here," says
the LORD,
"That My people are taken away for
nothing?
Those who rule over them
Make them wail," says the LORD.
"And My name is blasphemed continually
every day."

We find six horrible results of prayerless-
ness:

(1) Because we do not awake, we will sell ourselves to the devil for nothing.
(2) We will go down to Egypt, back into the
world.
(3) We will become oppressed.
(4) We will be taken away like slaves.
(5) We will wail and howl from the bondage we
are in.
(6) The wicked will blaspheme God, a condition
we see in our own country today because we
Christians do not pray.

And at that point, Isaiah shifts back to the good
results of awaking, or praying. He quotes God,
saying:

Therefore My people shall know My name;
Therefore they shall know in that day
That I am He who speaks;
"Behold, it is I" (Isa. 52:6).

Essentially, he says that as a seventh blessing
from true prayer, we shall know God and His
power.

Finally, the one who pays the price will be used
for the greatest possible service to the Lord, in
the words of Isaiah 52:7:

How beautiful upon the mountains
Are the feet of him who brings good news,
Who proclaims peace,
Who brings glad tidings of good things,
Who proclaims salvation,
Who says to Zion,
"Your God reigns!"

A Time for Decision

Once I understood through the teaching of the
Holy Spirit that the price Miss Kuhlman had been
talking about hinged simply on "awake, awake"
— in other words, prayer — I made the decision
that I would pay the price. I knew at last that
I had the answer to what she had been talking

about when she said, "If you find the power, you'll find heaven's treasure."

The decision to pay the price and to pray is something every Christian must decide for himself; no one can decide it for him. Paul wrote poignantly in 1 Corinthians 9:27: "I discipline my body and bring it into subjection, lest, when I have preached to others, I myself should become disqualified" [or "become a castaway," KJV].

God gives us all the opportunity to pray and calls us to it, but He will not force us. The choice is ours.

The second you say no to prayer — "I'm too tired" or "I don't feel like it" — the real you is an idol worshiper. You have submitted to the lower nature, and your flesh has taken the place of God.

You really need to understand that. God loves you. He will help you. But He will not force you. The Lord always leads, but the devil always pushes. It's up to you to take that flesh by the neck and say, "No, I'm going to pray!"

The awful danger of submitting to the flesh is revealed in the early chapters of Genesis. God made man (and woman) a being of spirit, soul, and body, but the devil, through the temptation of Eve and Adam, turned man around: body, soul, and spirit.

The flesh prevailed, and we find these tragic words in Genesis 6:3: "And the LORD said, 'My Spirit shall not strive with man forever, for he is indeed flesh.' " The devil had turned man upside down.

Submitting to the flesh is rebelling against God. It will kill you, and that is what you do when you refuse to pray. God will not use a man who has been turned upside down, and He certainly will not anoint him.

Start seeking God. Pay the price. Turn your life right side up, and He will anoint your head clear down to your feet.

God's telephone number is Jeremiah 33:3, and He's waiting for you: "Call to Me, and I will answer you, and show you great and mighty things, which you do not know."

He promises that, if you call on Him: First, He will answer; He will speak to you. Second, He will give you new vision and you will see His glory. Third, He will give you new knowledge, things you have never known about Him.

Chapter 5

It's Not By Might

Laying hands on the sick for the first time in my ministry was an amazing experience. I knew the Lord had told me to pray for the sick as part of preaching the gospel, just as He told the disciples, in Mark 16:18: "They will lay hands on the sick, and they will recover."

But this was new to me, and the devil had been filling my head with garbage for some time. In fact, I was standing at the bus stop on my way to preach for the second time, planning to lay hands on the sick, when he spoke quite specifically into my thoughts: "Nothing will happen. Nobody is going to get healed. It's not going to happen — nothing — nothing!"

As you might expect, I got this terrible feeling, this fear that the anointing would not come. But I couldn't stop then.

At the meeting, the anxiety still had a grip on me as I preached and invited the people to come forward for healing. In the early years,

I normally prayed for people one at a time, contrary to the way most of my miracle meetings are done these days.

So here was this fellow, waiting for me to pray. I had this terrible feeling; I was scared. "Where are you, Lord?" I thought. "What am I going to do? You said to do this."

I moved my hand toward the fellow's face and instantly the anointing of the Holy Spirit came. I knew it. He wobbled, and down he went as the power of the Holy Spirit went through him. He was healed of his ailment.

As I noted in the account of my first venture into preaching the gospel and the instant healing of my stutter, God is never early, but He is never late. It's as though He doesn't show up until your hand is poised above the person or until your mouth is open to speak. Just about the time you think you're going to die, He shows up.

Why? He's stretching your faith. He's building you up for the more difficult tasks ahead. James says that "the testing of your faith produces patience" — or endurance and perseverance — and that you should "let patience have its perfect work, that you may be perfect and complete, lacking nothing" (James 1:3-4).

You'll never know the stress I underwent in those early lessons. I often wanted to go home. "Oh, God," I would think, "they're going to laugh at me. I'm going to make a mess."

And then the anointing would come, for a lot of testing and maturing was needed if I was going

59

to become the man God intended.

It's the same way with you. As you prepare for the presence and the anointing of the Holy Spirit for whatever work the Lord has called you to, you will need testing and stretching and perfecting. Yesterday's anointing will not be today's anointing.

The Blessing of Silence

There was always a lot of singing in Kathryn Kuhlman's services, and she often would join in with great gusto and joy. And then there were times when she'd say to the audience, "Quietly, now, quietly." I would find myself wondering why she did that.

Then one time when I was there, she said, "Everybody, just quiet, please." It was clear she was serious, and everybody got very quiet. Charlie, the organist, played ever so softly; no one could play for her like Charlie. Everything else, and everyone, was quiet.

That went on for about ten minutes. Silence. Then this fellow seated near the front began to whisper into his hands, which were cupped over his mouth and nose, "Praise You, Jesus. Praise You, Jesus." I didn't think anyone could hear him, and I'm sure he wasn't even aware of it.

Immediately Miss Kuhlman spoke emphatically, "Sir, I said quiet!" Absolute silence returned, except for Charlie.

Minutes passed. And at last she said, barely audibly, just a whisper, "He comes in when you're quiet." She repeated it, even softer: "He comes in when you're quiet."

Man, I was scared. I didn't know what was going to happen, but I waited . . . and waited . . . and waited . . .

And then it happened!

All over the auditorium, miracles began to take place, which were confirmed in the next hour as Miss Kuhlman talked to the people in front of everyone else.

I had been in the ministry only three months, and I had never seen anything like it. Miracles were taking place all over the auditorium. And they began during silence.

I went back to Canada and thought about it. "I'm going to try this," I said. After all, I had already learned and experienced so much from Kathryn's meetings. God certainly used her for miracles all over the world, and He used her, graciously and mercifully, to teach and inspire me in those early days.

In my early days of ministry, I had a wild and wonderful choir, more than half of which were Jamaicans and Haitians and the rest a mixture of all backgrounds. And they were enthusiastic, to say the least. They were beautiful, but they could be noisy in their exuberance when worshiping the Lord.

So this one Monday night — the hall was packed — I said in advance that I would want them to be quiet at the crucial moment. Well, it took me

61

twenty minutes to get them quiet because they kept saying, "Thank you, Lord; Praise the Lord," the sort of thing that is perfectly normal for an excited, charismatic Christian.

I said, "Now quiet. If you want to move any more, I'm going to send you downstairs." And they did their best.

I looked over at my song leader, and his face told me he was wondering what in the world was going on. Quite frankly, about that time I was wondering myself what I was doing. I honestly didn't know whether I was doing something right or not. All I knew was that Kathryn had done it, and the Lord had acted. I figured that if nothing happened, I'd forget it and move on. "Get very quiet," I repeated to everyone.

So it took the choir twenty minutes to get quiet. Then it got quiet all over the room. It was really quiet. I didn't know what to do next, so I waited and stayed quiet. Pretty soon forty minutes had passed. I waited with my eyes shut because I had no idea what was going to happen — if anything. And after all that time, I didn't want to look.

Then *bang!* What was that? Then another bang, and another one, seemingly all over the auditorium. I couldn't resist opening my eyes. Three people in different parts of the room had fallen. And while I was looking, two more went down.

Then *whoosh!* Something filled the hall. I felt a strong electrical charge, like what I think a bolt of lightning would be. I felt a numbness sweep across most of my body. And right before my eyes, almost everyone there crumbled to the floor. Virtually no one was standing but me.

I was stunned. My song leader lay on the floor weeping. The musicians, the ushers, everyone was down. I grasped the pulpit tightly, and I heard the voice of God; I know I was the only one who did at that moment: "I left you standing to see it."

I had learned a lesson.

But God wasn't finished.

A few days later a friend named Peter called. It was Friday night and he said, "I want to take you somewhere tomorrow, but you have to be ready by five o'clock in the morning."

I never had liked early morning hours. "What for?" I asked.

"Never mind. I'll pick you up at five."

It was a hard struggle, but Peter was a good friend. I met him at five, and we headed off in his car. You don't have to drive far out of Toronto to be in the woods, and that's where we were shortly.

He parked and we walked several minutes into the forest. I mean, we were deep in the woods — secluded, with nothing but trees, birds, and squirrels.

We stopped, and he said, "I'll be right back."

I figured he needed to go to the bathroom, so I stood waiting. And I waited. And I waited. Ten minutes, twenty minutes. It was very quiet, and I began hearing sounds I'd never heard before. I could even hear my own heart pounding. I was sure I could hear my ears. It was very quiet.

I figured he should have been back by now. He hadn't just gone to the bathroom.

So I screamed, as loudly as I could: "Peeeeeeeterrrr."

More silence. And then suddenly he jumped from behind a bush — and scared me to death!

"That's why I brought you out here!" he said.

"To scare me?"

"No. To teach you that you don't know how to be quiet. You're always talking, or moving around and making noise. I brought you to the woods to teach you."

I wasn't impressed, or at least I said I wasn't.

"Do you know," Peter said, "that D.L. Moody said, 'If I can take an unbeliever and get him quiet for five minutes, and in those minutes have him think about eternity, I can get him saved. I won't have to say anything.' "

Quietness. I learned of its power. The Holy Place is quiet. You must learn to get still before God and worship Him quietly. You will discover the anointing.

Keeping the Promise

As I've said for many years, Kathryn Kuhlman was a minister of the gospel whom I followed very closely. Without even knowing it, she taught me so much.

But I must confess that the first time I saw her, in Pittsburgh, I wasn't nearly as appreciative as

I am now. From the third row of the First Presbyterian Church's sanctuary, I watched her glide, almost tiptoeing, onto the platform, arms wide, as she swept along in her floor-length, lacy, flowing gown with long sleeves and high neck. Then as the packed crowd erupted with "How Great Thou Art," this slender, auburn-haired lady literally ran to center stage, leading the conclusion of the powerful song quite loudly, which was one of the hallmarks of her amazing ministry.

The first words she spoke into the microphone were: "Helloooooooo therererere. And have you been waiaiaiaiaiaiting fooooooorrrrrr me?"

Regrettably, my under-the-breath response was a blunt "no." But I wasn't alone as one who stumbled over many of Miss Kuhlman's mannerisms. There's a lesson to be learned from the Bible's warnings against scorning. For I was among the relatively few who had the opportunity to witness from fairly close that the outward showmanship in no way revealed the heart, spirit, and power of the woman. I learned much, and am still learning from the experiences.

In my time around her ministry, I never saw her fail to speak, with tears in her eyes and an almost undetectable quiver of her lip, these words as she called upon the Lord: "I promise You the glory, and I thank You for this. I thank You for this." Sometimes it was just a very simple and intimate "Dear Jesus, thanks a million!"

I promise you, beloved, there can be no other way. As you seek and receive the anointing, the glory must be given to no one but the Lord. Any failure in this regard will be disastrous. I urge you only to think of the fallen ministers of God over many years who have stumbled at this point. Showmanship, even flamboyance, is one thing. Pride and ingratitude are another. "I promise You the glory, and, dear Jesus, thanks a million."

A Lesson About Prayer

In 1977, after Miss Kuhlman's passing in early 1976, I was asked by the Kuhlman Foundation to hold a memorial service for her in Pittsburgh. Up to that time, my work for her ministry had consisted of minor things like passing out choir music, so I was stunned that I would be asked to participate in such a significant event. I was very young and immature as a Christian, and this was going to be a major event.

When I arrived at the offices in the Carlton House, Maggie Hartner, who had been Kathryn's closest confidante and whom I love very much, took me aside and said something that amazed me.

"Now, don't go and pray and get so tied up and wrapped up in your own needs that God can't use you tonight," she said quite sternly. "Go take a nap or something."

I couldn't believe what I was hearing. "That is the most unspiritual thing I've ever heard," I thought, "and this is the most unspiritual woman I've ever met." I was going to go and pray whether she liked it or not.

66

Jimmy McDonald, the singer, picked me up and took me to the Carnegie Music Hall, describing the program for the evening. The choir would sing this and this, he said, and then he would sing. "When I begin leading, 'Jesus, There's Something About That Name,' you come out." I nodded okay.

Well, they showed a film of Kathryn's powerful service in Las Vegas, which continues to have a major impact when it's shown, then Jimmy sang.

I looked at the crowd from backstage and I froze. I couldn't move.

Jimmy sang the song a second time, and then a third time, and finally said, "When we sing this the next time, Benny Hinn is going to come out." He added a few complimentary words about me. Most people didn't know who I was, of course.

He sang again. I was still frozen with fright.

Finally I got out onto the stage. Jimmy whispered, "Where were you?" And he left the stage. That didn't make it any easier.

I tried to lead them into singing the song again, but I started too high, and it was terrible. Nobody sang with me. I was struggling by myself. All I could think about was getting out of there and going home.

It seemed like nearly half an hour had passed. All I could do was throw my arms up in the air and cry, "I can't do it, Lord; I can't do it."

At that moment, I heard a voice deep inside that said, "I'm glad you can't; now I will."

I totally relaxed, and it was like going from hell to heaven. There was instant release once I knew beyond a shadow of doubt that I couldn't do it. The power of God descended, and everyone in the hall was touched — not by me, but by God. It was a marvelous, moving service.

Maggie came to me later and said something that I will never forget: "Kathryn always said, 'It's not your prayers, it's not your ability, it's your surrender.' Learn how to surrender, Benny."

By then I was so stunned by the whole experience that I could only say, "Maggie, I don't think I know how."

"Well, you had your first experience tonight," she said.

Back at the hotel room, I prayed, "Lord, teach me how to do this." I knew the key was in Maggie's statement that afternoon. But only in the last few years have I fully understood what she was saying: Don't pray just because you have a service. I don't talk to my wife just when I need her. I'm supposed to have a relationship with her. It's the same with the Lord. You pray — all the time — so your fellowship can remain. You can't say, "I'll talk to You when I need You," and then ignore Him for a while. God will say, "No relationship, no anointing."

Your life depends on prayer.

A Matter of Trust

I know Maggie Hartner had this matter of relationship and trust in mind at the time of this very personal story I want to share with you. I know you'll understand.

Maggie and I were driving through the streets of Pittsburgh late one night after a service. The streets were deserted, and when we came to a stoplight, Maggie turned to me and said, "Do you see that building there on the left? This is where Miss Kuhlman and I lived for so many years in the early days."

It was rather an old apartment building. After a moment's silence, I said to her, "Maggie, tell me what Kathryn was like in those days."

As Maggie thought for a moment, the anointing of the Holy Spirit came upon her and it was as though God had stepped into the car. And she said: "Benny, I'm going to tell you something right now . . . and don't ever forget it."

Maggie was a powerful person, and she had my full attention. "You have a lot more than she had when she was your age. The power of God that you saw on Kathryn was only on her in the last ten years of her life."

I was stunned. "Maggie, I thought Kathryn always had that anointing."

"On no," she said. "In the earlier days she didn't have any anointing on her compared to what she had when she died."

Then she looked sharply at me in the dim light. "Do you know why God anointed her the way He did?"

I shook my head.

"Because He could trust her with it."

There were several seconds of silence. And she

pointed the forefinger of her right hand directly at my face and said evenly but forcefully: "And if He can trust you" — I felt as though God were talking to me — "if He can only trust you."

Her finger held steady in my face for a moment, and everything was stone silent as we drove on through the dark streets.

In my hotel that night, I could hardly talk. I was shaken. I spoke as seriously as I ever had in my life: "Lord, please make me an anointed man You can trust."

Trust.

"I promise You the glory, and, dear Jesus, thanks a million."

There is no other way.

Chapter 6

An Unusual Woman of God

Because of the number of young adults I've encountered who know very little about Kathryn Kuhlman, I want to tell you briefly about this remarkable woman who had such an impact on my life and who touched so many lives around the world. From what God did in her life, we can learn more about what He can do in ours through the anointing.

Born on May 9, 1907, near Concordia, Missouri, Kathryn grew into a tall, red-haired teenager, mischievous, strong-willed, and bright. She accepted Jesus as her Lord at age fourteen under the ministry of a Baptist evangelist during a typical Midwestern revival meeting at a small Methodist church. The experience in many ways was a forecast of the years to come. Stunning her family, church, and everyone in town, she was overcome by the Holy Spirit, sobbing, shaking, and collapsing under great conviction in a front pew.

"The whole world changed," she said years later. I could fully identify with the sobbing and shaking.

Only a few years after her conversion she joined her sister Myrtle and Myrtle's husband on an evangelistic road trip, and before long, feeling an increasing burden for the lost, she set out on her own traveling ministry. Accompanied by pianist Helen Gulliford, she ministered throughout the Midwest and West for several years, finally landing in Denver, where she soon attracted large crowds to meetings held in a warehouse.

Out of those meetings in 1933, at the height of the Depression, came the Denver Revival Tabernacle, a major work that flourished. During this time, she was pretty much a preacher of the gospel, bringing hundreds and hundreds of people to the Lord. Although healings through prayer occurred as in many Christian ministries, her powerful miracle ministry was a long way off. But near-disaster was close at hand. Fortunately God had a plan to overcome Kathryn's weaknesses.

In 1937 she invited a tall, handsome evangelist named Burroughs Waltrip to minister at the Tabernacle. He stayed for two months. Although he was still married, he had left his wife and children in a most odious fashion. Kathryn lost all sound judgment and fell in love with him. When he finally divorced his wife, Kathryn married him, despite pleadings and warnings from those who cared for her. She then followed Waltrip to Iowa.

Her booming ministry collapsed, although parts of the Denver work continued under other leaders.

Waltrip's ministry also failed in Iowa. So they left and traveled extensively around the Midwest and west, sometimes ministering together, but more often she sat silently on the platform as he ministered. Because of the grace of God, people were often saved and blessed under their ministry, but the life went out of both of them, especially her.

Kathryn had walked away from her first real love, the Lord Jesus Christ, and she was dying. According to Jamie Buckingham, an author and pastor, she had known for many years that she was to be different. The call on her was so deep, so irreversible, that after about six years she could stand her misery no longer. Waltrip knew it, too, but it was Kathryn who acted.

In *Daughter of Destiny*, a book Buckingham wrote about Miss Kuhlman after her death, he quoted her on this critical transition in her life:

I had to make a choice. Would I serve the man I loved or the God I loved? I knew I could not serve God and live with Mister. [She called Waltrip "Mister" from the very first time she met him.] No one will ever know the pain of dying like I know it, for I loved him more than I loved life itself. And for a time, I loved him even more than God. I finally told him I had to leave. God had never released me from that original call. Not

73

only did I live with him, I had to live with my own conscience, and the conviction of the Holy Spirit was almost unbearable. I was tired of trying to justify myself. Tired. One afternoon, I left the apartment — it was in the outskirts of Los Angeles — and found myself walking down a tree-shaded street. The sun was flickering through the great limbs that stretched out overhead. At the end of the block I saw a street sign. It said simply, "Dead End." There was heartache, heartache so great it cannot be put into words. If you think it's easy to go to the cross, it's simply because you've never been there. I've been there. I know. And I had to go alone. I knew nothing about the wonderful filling of the Holy Spirit. I knew nothing of the power of the mighty third person of the Trinity which was available to all. I just knew it was four o'clock on Saturday afternoon and I had come to the place in my life where I was ready to give up everything — even Mister — and die. I said it out loud: "Dear Jesus, I surrender all. I give it all to you. Take my body. Take my heart. All I am is yours. I place it in your wonderful hands."

Kathryn had known for almost six years that she had been fooling herself. She had been preaching and seeking God's blessing without living under God's precepts. She had sinned. But she repented, turning around that Saturday afternoon.

She died. She became a seed willing to fall into the ground and be buried. In the words of Buckingham, "She turned around and started back up the street whence she had come." And she was alone, except for a loving, forgiving God. "No one," she cried softly many years later, "will ever know what this ministry has cost me. Only Jesus."

I discussed Kathryn's "dying" with Maggie Hartner years later, and she gave me great insight — insight that we must all learn from. At that time of repentance and turning around, Kathryn was understandably grief-stricken and guilt-ridden. The Lord, at one point, asked her, "Kathryn, have I forgiven you?" She answered, "Yes." Then God said, "I have forgotten it, and in My book it never happened."

From that moment on, until late in her life, she never spoke of the matter, treating it as God said He had.

According to the Scripture, God has put repented sins behind Him and never looks at them. They are as far from him as the East is from the West. If you keep coming back and asking for forgiveness, He really doesn't know what you are talking about. Repentance. The washing of the blood. Forgiveness. A clean slate. Who was Kathryn Kuhlman that she should treat sin in a way contrary to God? It never happened.

The Door Opens

Two years later, after many ups and downs and many rejections because she was a woman who had married a divorced man, Miss Kuhlman got off the bus in Franklin, in western Pennsylvania. The door was at last ready to open.

She began a lengthy stay at the Gospel Tabernacle and during that time started a radio ministry that was to prosper and, by stages, reach out across America. She eventually landed in Pittsburgh, which was to be the headquarters for her amazing ministry.

During the time in Franklin, she began to wrestle with the issue of healing. She sometimes preached on healing, and people would be healed, but it was not a major emphasis in her ministry, which was designed to lead people to rebirth through Christ. "I knew in my heart that there was healing," she told Buckingham many years later. "I had seen the evidence from those who had been healed. It was real, and it was genuine, but what was the key?"

One day she saw an ad for a tent meeting in Erie that featured a "healing evangelist" and decided to go. Maybe she would find the key. But it was not there, at least for her. The evangelist was loud, brassy, and acrobatic, which was the furthest thing from her ministry. The audience seemed to go crazy as he yelled; they screamed, wailed, and writhed. She saw evidence of fraud in the claims of healing, and she could only weep. People were being criticized for their lack of faith, which left them in despair and hopelessness.

But Kathryn, as brokenhearted as she was, still believed the Word of God, and she turned to it for help.

The upshot was that on April 27, 1947, she began a teaching series on the Holy Spirit. I want to reprint portions of that teaching, as found in Buckingham's book, for it contained truth that was to shape Miss Kuhlman's ministry for the rest of her life:

I see in my mind the three persons of the Trinity sitting down at a great conference table before the formation of the earth took place. God, the Holy Father, gave the others the news that even though He would create men to have fellowship with Him, that man would sin — and break that fellowship. The only way fellowship could be restored would be for someone to pay the price for that sin. For if another did not pay it, then man himself would have to continue to pay the price in unhappiness, disease, death, and eventual hell. After the Holy Father finished sharing, His Son Jesus spoke up and said, "I'll go. I'll take the form of a man and go down to earth to pay that price. I'll be willing to die on a cross so that man can be restored to perfect fellowship with us." Then Jesus turned to the Holy Spirit and said, "But I cannot go unless You go with me — for You are the one with the power." The Holy Spirit responded and said, "You go ahead. And when the time is right, I shall join You on earth." So Jesus came to earth, born in a manger, and grew to manhood. But even though He was the very Son of God, He was powerless. Then came that magnificent moment at the River Jordan when Jesus, coming up out of the baptismal waters, looked up and saw the Holy Spirit descending upon Him in the form of a dove. It must have been one of the greatest thrills Jesus received as He walked in the flesh on this earth. And I can almost hear the Holy Spirit whisper in His ear, "I'm here now. We're running right on schedule. Now things will really happen." And they did happen. Filled with the Spirit, He was suddenly empowered to heal the sick, cause the blind to see, even raise the dead. It was the time for miracles. For three years they continued, and then, at the end, the Bible says He "gave up the ghost," and the Spirit returned to the Holy Father. After Jesus was in the grave for three days, that mighty third person of the Trinity, the Holy Spirit, returned. Jesus came out of the grave in a glorified body. He performed no more miracles during the short time He was here, but He gave His followers a great promise — the greatest promise of all, the Bible. He said that same Holy Spirit who had lived in Him would return to live in all those who opened their lives to His power. The same things that He, Jesus, had done, His followers would do also. In fact, even greater things would be done because now the Holy Spirit would not be limited to one body — but would be free to enter all those everywhere who would receive Him. The last words [Jesus] said before He went away were, "And ye shall receive power after the Holy Ghost is come upon you." God the Father had given Him the gift. Now He was passing it on to the church. Every church should be experiencing the miracles of Pentecost. Every church should be seeing the healings of the Book of Acts. The gift is for all of us.

The Reaction Is Fast

The following night, as Kathryn stood to preach, a woman rushed toward the front with her hand raised. "Kathryn, may I say something?" she asked.

Miss Kuhlman, not used to this sort of interruption, still said in the manner thousands would grow to love, "Come on, honey, of course you can say something."

"Last night, while you were preaching I was healed," she said softly.

Kathryn, probably for the only time in her life, was speechless. She hadn't touched or seen the woman, let alone prayed for her.

"Where were you?" she managed to ask.

"Just sitting there in the audience."

Kathryn said, "How do you know you were healed?"

"I had a tumor. It had been diagnosed by my doctor. While you were preaching, something happened in my body. I was so sure I was healed that I went back to my doctor this morning and had it verified. The tumor is no longer there."

The miraculous anointing had come.

Another healing occurred the following Sunday, and the following, and the following, on and on, as the power of God surged through her ministry until the Lord took her home in 1976.

All of us are not called or empowered to heal others as Kathryn did. But if we are willing to give God everything, regardless of the cost, He will anoint our lives, directing us to do great works for Him through the power of His magnificent Spirit.

Are you willing to pay the price? Remember, you can't outgive God. Whatever you release and give over to Him, He will return through the anointing more than you could ever imagine.

Chapter 7

What Is It?

People find many indescribable teachings and truths in the Bible. One pertains to the glory of God, but what is this glory?

Some associate the glory with an intimate experience they may have had — an experience in which God seemed so close. But they fumble for words when trying to explain it.

The truth is that the glory of God is the person and presence of God — the glory is the Holy Spirit. When you experience His presence — the overwhelming realization that God Almighty is so near you can almost reach out and touch Him — then you have experienced the glory of God. You feel the warmth of His love, the comfort of His peace. This is an anointing, in a sense, of course — an anointing that brings the presence.

The wonderful experience of the presence causes you to wonder: "Who am I that You, the Creator of the universe, would allow me to be in Your presence?" It's the same question David the psalmist asked:

> *When I consider Your heavens, the work of*
>   *Your fingers,*
> *The moon and the stars, which You have*
>   *ordained,*
> *What is man that You are mindful of him,*
> *And the son of man that You visit him?*
>   *(Ps. 8:3-4)*

You are in total awe as you experience the presence and glory of God. How can God be great enough to create everything there is and yet small enough, if you will, and near enough for you — a speck of dust that He breathed into — to know the intimacy of His presence and love? You feel as though you have been ushered into the throne room of heaven and given a private audience with God. His arms seem to enfold you and wrap you in His love. The cares of the world pass away.

But there is more. When the presence of God comes, the attributes of God come as well. Think of the experience of Moses, as found in Exodus 33:18ff.

"Please, show me Your glory," he said. Note the request: He asked to *see* God's glory, believing that it could be experienced and known.

And God replied, "I will make all my goodness pass before you, and I will proclaim the name of the Lord before you. I will be gracious to whom I will be gracious, and I will have compassion on whom I will have compassion."

Goodness, mercy, and compassion were to be shown to him in a concrete, visible way. With the presence would come the nature — the very attributes of God Himself. Look at what happened a few verses later:

> Then the LORD descended in the cloud and stood with him there, and proclaimed the name of the LORD. And the Lord passed before him and proclaimed: "The LORD, the Lord GOD, merciful and gracious, longsuffering, and abounding in goodness and truth, keeping mercy for thousands, forgiving iniquity and transgression and sin, by no means clearing the guilty, visiting the iniquity of the fathers upon the children and the children's children to the third and the fourth generation."

The glory, or the presence, comes and so do the attributes: grace, mercy, forgiveness, compassion, goodness.

Lives are changed for eternity. In short the Holy Spirit brings the fruit of the Spirit, as described in Galatians 5:22-23. And the fruit must come before the anointing for service comes.

Then There Is Power

Yes, the presence of God is His glory, His personality, His attributes. The Holy Spirit, God, is a person who wants lovingly and yearningly to make His presence known to you. And it is possible, now and forever, to live in that presence.

I want you to experience the truth that the presence of the Holy Spirit can and should lead to the anointing for service. The presence must precede the anointing.

What is this anointing? *It is the power of God.*

Say it aloud: *The anointing is the power of God.*

Simple? Yes — even though we're talking about power that exceeds anything man can generate. It is the power that brought the heavens and the earth into being. It is the power that created man. It is the power that raised Jesus from the dead. It is the power that will bring Jesus from the right hand of God to earth at the appointed time and will cause all things to be made new.

I want you to understand: The presence of God the Holy Spirit leads to the anointing of the Spirit, which is the power of God, and the power of God brings forth the manifestation of the presence. The anointing itself — an anointing of the Holy Spirit — cannot be seen, but the power, its manifestations, its effects, can and should be seen. That is why I call it "the tangible anointing." This, of course, harmonizes with the Lord's teaching to Nicodemus in John 3:8 that the Spirit blows like the wind, in which case its effects can be seen.

Beyond the salvation message itself, the most explosive words of the Scripture came out of Christ's mouth as recorded in Acts 1:8. They are vital to the truth of the anointing:

But ye shall receive power, after that the Holy Ghost is come upon you: and ye shall be witnesses

84

unto me both in Jerusalem, and in all Judaea, and in Samaria, and unto the uttermost part of the earth. (KJV)

Amazing! You shall receive power — the anointing, the spiritual gifts — after the Holy Ghost — the presence, the person, the fruit — comes upon you.

Do you see it? The fruit of the Spirit, so missing in the church today, is connected to the *presence* of God. The gifts and ministry of God, also sadly missing, are connected to the *power* of God.

What are fruits? They are qualities or characteristics — attributes — of a person, in this case God. They begin *inside* you, where God is if you're a believer. God says, "I will come in, and My fruit will come in with Me. I leave, and My fruit will go with Me."

Not so with power. The power of God comes *upon* you, as a gift. It stays with you. As Paul wrote to the Romans, speaking of the current and future conditions of the Jews: "The gifts and the calling of God are irrevocable" (Rom. 11:29). Yes, it is not an easy truth, but it is possible for the presence to withdraw and the gifts to remain, at least for a while. But that will ultimately lead to disaster.

God Is Not Divided

The fruits of the Spirit, which come with the presence, are not progressive; they are instant. There is nothing to suggest that the fruits enter your life and then "grow." Remember, they are not *your* fruits or attributes; they are *God's.* And He doesn't divide Himself up when He enters you. Neither does He grow up in You. He comes in with fullness. Righteous characteristics should and can shine from your life right then. You get all of Him!

His fruits, therefore, should shine forth from you when you become His ambassador. They should touch and affect each life you reach out to, for it takes more than boldness and a loud voice to be an ambassador of the gospel to the world.

Stop for a moment and think. Think honestly. Is this the case in your life? If not, the issue is not the anointing and the power. The issue is the presence of the Holy Spirit. Are you experiencing Him day by day, moment by moment?

I'm sure some of you are saying, "Come on, Benny! The fruits take time to develop."

No, my friend; you are wrong. Look at Paul the apostle, previously called Saul, a man felled by the Spirit of God on the road to Damascus. He fell and came out a new man. He had been a murderer, and immediately after his experience with the presence of God the Son through God the Holy Spirit, he was no longer a killer. Prior to that, he had had no genuine knowledge of God. Suddenly, however, he knew God and lived for Him. He was even willing to die for Him. It did not take him ten years to change.

Paul was under the power and heard God's voice. Ezekiel was under the power and heard God's voice. Why? Because the Lord was present, and He produced virtue. Throughout Scripture there are similar cases.

My friend, the voice of God is heard in His presence, and this enables you under the anointing to speak *your words* that produce results. Let me say it again: The presence of God carries *His* voice; the gifts of God carry *yours*. Thus, in Acts 1:8, Jesus said the empowered disciples would be His *witnesses*. The power was for service, not merely goosebumps.

Power from the Start

Christians tend to think of the Holy Spirit in the context of the New Testament only, and that is a mistake. The tremendous power of the Holy Spirit was manifest in creation, as well as at other times in redemptive history. Genesis 1:2 tells us that when the earth was without form and void and darkness was on the face of the deep, "the Spirit of God was hovering over the face of the waters." The Holy Spirit was present at Creation as part of the Godhead, being the first manifestation of God on earth. He will always be the first manifestation in your life.

As we study the anointing of the Holy Spirit, which is the power of God, I want you always to remember who the Spirit is. Sometimes He's represented as a dove, but He is not a dove. Sometimes He is pictured as a flame of fire, but He is not fire. Sometimes He's seen as oil or water or wind, but He is none of these.

He is a spirit being. But even with no physical form, He is a person more real than you or me. He is the power of the Godhead.

Isn't it odd that, throughout history, man has sought power and yet today, as previously, men and women generally try to build and show their own power rather than embrace the truest and greatest power there is? They were trying it at the time of the tower of Babel (Genesis 11), and they're still trying. When God's mighty shaking occurs (Heb. 12:26), mankind's greatest power will crumble like dirt.

The combined strength of every nuclear bomb made in this frightened world, the combined strength of every flood and hurricane to strike the globe, the combined strength of Satan and every demon slave of his are as the weakest firecracker compared with the power of Almighty God, Creator of heaven and earth.

Now, beloved, that is the power with which our Lord wants to clothe you.

Despite the rebellion against God found in much of general society, millions of people like you are hungering for the reality found in the real God. That is why our monthly miracle crusades around the United States are drawing overflow crowds at each site. When we seat about fifteen thousand enthusiastic believers, we are forced to turn away around four thousand disappointed seekers. You see, God has chosen to move with extraordinary power in our time, honoring the preaching of the gospel with signs and wonders, as He said in Scripture He would do. This obviously is a very important time in history, and we — all of us — need the anointing of the Holy Spirit to fulfill the roles He is calling us to. And I am totally optimistic. He will do what He promised.

The purpose of this book is to help meet that need in your life.

Chapter 8

You Must Have It

The anointing is a must if you want to be used by God, no matter what position you're in. It carries a heavier responsibility than the presence of God by itself, but you cannot do without it.

His presence can be yours and you can have fellowship with Him regularly, loving Him, walking with Him, without even having a ministry. But the second you step into the ministry, you need the power to fight devils, sickness, and the powers of hell. No matter what your ministerial calling is, you need the power of the anointing to fulfill it. You will never accomplish what God wants you to do without it.

I am not overstating the case. The anointing is mandatory if you are called to serve the Lord. Without it there will be no growth, no blessing, no victory in your ministry.

You see, as harsh as it sounds, I can have the wonderful presence of God in my life — and I wouldn't trade it for anything — and I can stand behind a pulpit and minister. But if there is no power, I will be the only one having a good time. The people will see absolutely nothing. True, they may feel His presence, but we all should be feeling that as Christians. There will be no salvations, no healings, no binding of devils. The power is essential.

Remember how I have emphasized these words of the Lord just before His ascension: "Ye shall receive power, after the Holy Ghost is come upon you; and ye shall be witnesses unto me." After the power came three thousand were saved, then another five thousand, and then all Jerusalem was shaken. That's the power you must have with any service to God. In tandem with the presence, it will be the greatest plus your life can have.

When I step behind the pulpit, I always say, "Lord, please anoint me today, or my words will be dead," and I know beyond any question that had the Lord chosen not to clothe me with His power, I would have no church. No lives would be changed, no souls saved, and no bodies healed.

An Increase Will Come

Now as you go on with the anointing God gives you, He will trust you with more. You see, the presence that came on me in 1973 in my room in Toronto hasn't changed. It's still the same presence. It's still the same marvelous intimacy. It's true that you do get closer to the Lord because you get to know Him better and He teaches you more, but it's the same presence.

On the other hand, the anointing increases. He gives you a little and watches you. Then He gives you more. But before He gives you more, there are additional lessons to learn, more battles to fight.

Every time the anointing is increased on me, for example, I will go through a period of learning new things about Him and His ways — why did this happen and why didn't that happen? I find endless growth and excitement.

In my case, from 1974 until 1980, with my own ministry in Canada and also ministry with the Kathryn Kuhlman Foundation, the main thing I learned was that the anointing was totally dependent upon my obedience. And that is absolutely pivotal. The anointing, the power, comes through obedience. What do you do with a little that He gives you? Obey, and it increases. Disobey, and it stops.

A good example occurred early in my ministry in Canada. I was sitting before a service and I knew, I just knew, that the Lord was about to do a new thing in my ministry. Somehow I knew I wasn't supposed to ask what. "Don't ask me;" that's all I heard.

As the service proceeded, I laid my hands on a person needing help, and nothing happened. A second person came up, and nothing happened — no falling under the power, nothing. After the third person, I was a nervous wreck.

Then something in me kept whispering, "Say,

'The power of the Spirit goes through you.' "

"Why should I say that?" The fourth person, nothing. Then the fifth one, nothing. And the suggestion was still there: "Say, 'The power of the Spirit goes through you.' "

Finally I began to get the idea. "Lord, are You teaching me something new?"

"Start doing what I'm telling you," He replied.

Finally the next person came up, and I said, "The power of the Spirit goes through you." *Bang!* Down he went. The next one the same; the next one; the next one.

"What is happening?" I asked myself.

Finally I realized that the anointing is dependent upon *my* words. God will not move unless I say it. Why? Because He has made us coworkers with Him. He set things up that way.

That lesson continued in those early days. At that time, people found healing, but not when they still sat in their seats. They would have to come forward, and I would lay hands on them before healing would come. But one day, I heard the voice inside: "Rebuke sickness publicly." I went through a dialog with the Lord similar to the example above and finally said aloud, "I rebuke every sickness in this place in Jesus' name."

The Lord said inside me, "Say it again."

I complied, "I rebuke every sickness in this place in Jesus' name."

"One more time," He said.

So I said it one more time. The most awesome thing happened. Instantly I knew someone in the balcony was being healed and I spoke it just as I heard it: "Somebody's hips and legs are being healed."

For the longest time there was no response and then, finally, a woman came down and said she was healed the second I said it.

From that point on, I began to learn that the anointing will not flow and touch anyone if I'm afraid. Boldness is a must. I must use the weapons He's given me, His words and His name. He said, "In My name, do it."

Now this is important: Those who try to use those weapons in His name and lack His presence and His anointing are fools. Anyone who pronounces, "By His stripes I am healed," and who doesn't have the presence, is wasting his time.

I want to state it again: The presence came into my life and had fellowship with me during that year when I was alone with the Holy Spirit in my room in Toronto. He helped me, comforted me, and taught me. After a while He gave me the authority, the power, to fulfill His word: "In My name they shall cast out devils" . . . "In my name they shall lay hands on the sick and they shall recover" . . . "In my name."

I was not speaking and acting in ignorance, but in knowledge and obedience. I knew Him and obeyed Him. That's the whole thing. If you have a relationship with Him and submit to His commands, His name will have power in your life. If you don't do this, you'll be mocked by devils. No, you must flow with the will of God in the service of God to obtain the power of God.

Of course, there have been times when I thought the Lord was going in one direction, and He wasn't. I went that wrong way and fell flat on my face every time. But I came right back, found the right way, and the anointing returned.

The Strongman Principle

In the 1980s I kept learning. I was with Reinhard Bonnke, the healing evangelist with an incredible ministry in Africa, and others who were serving the Lord in power. I learned a lot from them, and I still do.

For example, I heard Bonnke one day cry out, "You devil of blindness, I command you in Jesus' name to come out!"

"What's this?" I thought. I hadn't even known there was a devil of blindness. I couldn't remember having any blind people healed in my services, but he had blind people being healed right and left. "My," I asked myself, "is this true?"

So I tried such a command in my services, and more blind people were healed than I could have imagined possible.

Pressing ahead with study of the Scripture, I learned that the Lord always dealt with the strongmen. He never dealt with little demons, but always went after the big ones — the princes who had control over ordinary demons.

In my healing crusades, the Lord will often show me a strongman and I will address him head on: "You spirit of infirmity" . . . "You spirit of death." And that is when the miracles break forth. The power is incredible when I address the strongman and command, "In the name of Jesus, let the people go!" You can actually hear it. *Whoosh!* Power surges throughout the hall.

I've had people scream, taken completely by surprise, at the moment they are released and healed.

In this way I've learned more and more about the anointing. And this raises the point of knowledge of the Bible. The anointing is dependent on obedience, yes, but knowledge of Scripture is also key to that obedience. For the more you know about God, the more He can trust you with the power.

I often think of Miss Kuhlman's questions: "Do you really know Him? Do you know what grieves Him? Do you know what pleases Him?" And I think I can answer her, "Yes, Kathryn, I really do think I know Him." But I don't know Him fully yet — I'm still learning. I don't think I will ever quit learning, and I'm sure you will be the same.

Several times I have come to a point where I say, "I've got it," and then He has done something fresh and new. He is full of surprises. He will do things one way for quite a while, and then the anointing flows and He does it differently — never contrary to the Word, of course.

Laughter in Lisbon

During a service in Lisbon, Portugal, I learned something about the Lord that still amazes me. It centered around a woman forty to forty-five years of age, a typical mama with a scarf around her head, but quite emotionless, very quiet. I started to pray for her and the second I touched her, she fell under the power of the Spirit and went into incredible laughter. Her face turned red instantly, and she was beaming and laughing — not offensively, but beautifully.

Then she began to roll back and forth on the floor in ecstasy, totally transformed. This normal, down-to-earth woman, quiet, poker-faced, no makeup, plain, went into the most beautiful laughter I'd ever seen. And she rolled back and forth, back and forth. I told my assistants not to touch her, I was so moved I wanted to watch her and learn something new about the Holy Spirit. I was certain that the whole episode was too beautiful to be "in the flesh." I really wanted to stop her and ask, "What is happening to you?" but I couldn't. She was in such ecstasy.

When she finally stopped, she couldn't talk; she was simply overwhelmed. Finally she said through a translator, "It was impossible to describe." I desperately wished I could have spoken Portuguese, so I could have learned more.

The Lord taught me something new that day. I had heard Kathryn speak of holy laughter, but

I had never heard it. Since that lesson, I've seen it occur many times during ministry. When it is not in the flesh, which is ugly, it is a perfect example of ecstasy. I've yearned for the Lord to do that to me sometime, for He is truly wonderful in His great love for His people.

God Is the Boss

As I've said, my ministry took quantum leaps forward in 1990 when the Lord told me to begin monthly miracle crusades around the country, in addition to the regular pastoral ministry at the Orlando Christian Center.

There have been many extraordinary events. One that seems to happen in every crusade, usually in the teaching meetings on the morning of the second day, is the directive from the Lord to have the people get quiet, with eyes closed and hands raised. The Lord will tell me, "Say 'now' and I will touch them." That's all He tells me to do: "Say 'now.'"

It's amazing! I do it, and right away there will be gasps and even screams as the power falls. I open my eyes and invariably two thirds of the ten thousand or more present collapse onto the floor. Healings of all kinds occur, and God makes Himself powerfully known.

There are other ways in which the Spirit has poured freshness over us. For example, I began to notice that God was healing atheists. He was touching Protestants, Catholics, Pentecostals, non-

Pentecostals, charismatics, non-charismatics, everybody — even those who in my opinion weren't born again or living for the Lord or anything.

Obviously I must learn, and remember — like everyone else — that we can't limit God. We cannot tell Him who should receive miracles and who should not. And our love must be as inclusive as His.

I asked a well-known man of God why unbelievers were being healed, and he asked me, "Whom did Jesus heal?"

I had no reply other than, "You're right. He healed unbelievers."

Thus I have been learning — relearning — that we are dealing with the grace of God, not our own works. If He wants to have mercy on someone who comes to one of my meetings out of curiosity or perhaps to scoff, I can only say, "I'm still learning."

Chapter 9

Three Anointings

Scripture reveals three anointings of the Holy Spirit. Knowledge of them will help bring your potential as a Christian into focus.

The Leper's Anointing

First is *the leper's anointing*. Leviticus 14 teaches that the leper remained outside the camp and that the priest was to go out to him and apply the blood of the sacrifice, bring him into the camp, apply the blood again, and then apply oil, "making atonement for him before the Lord."

Every born-again believer has experienced the leper's anointing, which deals with salvation. Leprosy in this case is a type of sin, incurable in the natural world, but curable by God. Sin is the same; man can do nothing to remove it and its effects.

In the ceremonial cleansing of the Old Testament, the blood of the sacrificial animals was applied. In the New Testament, we find that the only cure for sin, then and today, is the blood of Jesus Christ. The animal sacrifices of Leviticus merely looked forward to the perfect sacrifice of the Lamb of God. They were a shadow; Jesus was the substance.

In John 1:29, John the Baptist sees Jesus approaching and declares, "Behold! The Lamb of God who takes away the sin of the world!" To those who came to know Him, Jesus was that Lamb of God. Jesus was the only sacrifice that would atone for the sin of the world.

In the ceremonial cleansing of Leviticus, the blood was applied, then the oil. The application of the sacrificial blood is symbolic of the blood of Christ, while the application of the oil is symbolic of the touch and influence of the Holy Spirit upon a life.

Just as the blood of Jesus Christ flows out to all who call upon His name, so the leper's anointing crosses all national and denominational barriers. For when anyone experiences the grace of Jesus Christ, it is the Holy Spirit who convicts him of sin and assures him of God's forgiveness.

Thus it is that at salvation you experience the first anointing — the leper's anointing — which reveals the power of the blood through the oil of anointing that pours over you.

The Priestly Anointing

As a believer, cleansed through the precious blood of Christ, born again and sealed by the Spirit, you can and should move to the second anointing: *the priestly anointing.* A significant number of believers have no knowledge of this level of the Holy Spirit's activity in their lives, and they certainly have no idea how to receive it. If you're among them, having no indication of such a blessing, read on, and you will discover and enter into God's additional anointing of power.

I must emphasize the importance of this step, since every member of the Body of Christ should have a ministry. And this is the anointing for ministry unto the Lord, including leading souls to Him, but not service of Him in battles against the devil and disease, but ministry to Him as priests. For we are all priests of God, although not necessarily ordained to stand behind a pulpit or to conduct evangelistic and healing services.

If we, therefore, are ministers to God, we must have the power of the Spirit to do so. And that means we are to be baptized in the Holy Spirit, which is the priestly anointing of the Holy Spirit upon us. Without it, we will accomplish little.

Also — and this is important — the priestly anointing is evidenced through unity in the Body of Christ as life in the Kingdom of God. All too often I have encountered self-appointed bearers of this anointing who are lone wolves. They think "their" callings and "their" ministries are so outstanding that they overlook the Body of Christ. They actually overlook God.

When the genuine priestly anointing has been experienced, there will be unity and harmony. Remember Psalm 133: "Behold, how good and how pleasant it is for brethren to dwell together in unity! It is like the precious oil upon the head, running down on the beard, the beard of Aaron, running down on the edge of his garments."

There is no such thing as a private priestly anointing; it comes in oneness, in unity, as the church functions as one body.

On the day of Pentecost in the book of Acts, 120 people were together — in one accord — in the Upper Room, and the Holy Spirit came upon them with fire and power. They went out from that room and ministered to the Lord, bearing witness to the crowds gathered there. Three thousand were saved! What an anointing! God was clearly present.

This priestly anointing is not a one-time anointing, which the leper's anointing is. Under the old covenant, the priests were anointed with oil every day. The same with you under the new covenant. You need a daily anointing.

The priestly anointing brings the presence, the communion, the fellowship of the Holy Spirit. Revelation knowledge comes, for in the leper's anointing, we are introduced to God in an extraordinary and wonderful way and we see our total need for Jesus Christ. But we really don't understand much more.

It is so sad that many Christians stay at the leper's anointing level, by choice. They don't seek more. They simply don't surrender. Their ears are dull; they don't hear God's voice.

And the Bible tells us clearly that Jesus said, "My sheep hear My voice." If you are truly one of His sheep and have received the priestly anointing, you will know His presence and hear the gentle voice of God regularly. It is not a one-time experience though; it must be renewed.

God sometimes will reveal incredible truths to you; at other times, He will just let you sense how much He loves you. Perhaps He will correct or instruct you on a matter; perhaps He will cause a particular passage of Scripture to stand out while you are reading His Word.

Even though you may seldom or never hear an audible voice, He has many avenues through which to speak to you. God's regular communication does not depend on how loudly He speaks but upon how well you listen. "He who has ears to hear, let him hear!" Matthew 11:15 says. You must take time each day to be quiet before the Lord so His still, small voice can be heard. As you read the Bible, fellowship with the Holy Spirit, and listen, you will experience that daily refreshing that keeps your heart ablaze with love for the Master.

The leper's anointing (salvation) is a one-time experience and cannot be lost unless you willfully walk away from it. God will never let you go unless you let Him go. This requires a decision that you would rather perish than be saved.

The priestly anointing (the presence), on the other hand, can be lost, for if sin comes into your heart it lifts. That is why it must be renewed daily; it will bring you into the presence of God — so near, so real that the tears will course down your cheeks.

The Kingly Anointing

Once you have experienced the leper's anointing and gone on to the priestly anointing, do not stop there. They are important and wonderful, but more is possible.

Nothing can compare with *the kingly anointing*, the most powerful of them all. This lifts a person to a place of high authority in God, giving him authority over devils, the power to rout demons with one word. Only this will give you the power to send the enemies of God flying as the apostle Paul did.

The kingly anointing is the most difficult to receive. Whereas the leper's anointing comes by *accepting Jesus* and the priestly anointing comes by *fellowship* with Jesus, the kingly anointing comes by *obeying* Jesus.

It is when you hear the *rhema* word of the Lord spoken just for that moment — which says, "Thus saith the Lord" — that you receive the kingly anointing. You see, there is the *logos*, or written Word — the Bible. But that does not give you the anointing, although the *logos* is terribly, terribly important, being settled in heaven and forever true.

Increase Comes at Crusades

This anointing became the most pronounced in my life when the Lord directed me in 1990 to begin monthly crusades around the country, which I have been doing ever since. I merely obeyed, and the extra anointing was there, although I have grown in it at a fast pace. I know the heavier anointing has come directly through obedience.

I had known this anointing before, but at the crusades I immediately began to receive power to drive out devils of sickness and affliction and to receive specific direction as to what the Holy Spirit was doing among the crowds of twelve to fifteen thousand that attended each night. Hundreds of verified healings and thousands of conversions have occurred, including people rising from wheelchairs and leaving crutches. Several blind eyes and deaf ears have been opened and verified.

In a crusade in Tulsa, Oklahoma, an Oklahoma City woman in a wheelchair was healed of what was described as failed back syndrome, with nerve damage and bone deformity, while on the platform in front of thousands of people. She reported having been told by her doctors at an Oklahoma City clinic that, because of nerve damage, she would never walk again. When checked sometime later she said she was "doing well" and without a wheelchair.

Also in Tulsa, where the anointing was very

heavy, a woman from Hobbs, New Mexico, diagnosed to have chronic leukemia by a doctor in Albuquerque, was healed and later possessed papers that said she was free of leukemia.

In my daily television program, which also resulted from a directive from the Lord at the time of the word to begin crusades, we show clips from the various crusades as well as pray for people directly. A Las Vegas woman, diagnosed to have lymphocytic leukemia, was healed watching the program. Her healing was confirmed by her doctor, who said he had never seen such a thing before, and her insurance company even dropped her rates when told of the confirmed healing.

And it goes on: In a Portland, Oregon, crusade, a woman from Milwaukee with a debilitating environmental illness (basically was an allergic reaction that blocked her vital organs) was healed, with the miracle confirmed by her doctor. In a Spartanburg, South Carolina, crusade a woman was healed of a serious disease in the chest cavity, with confirmation from her doctor.

And every bit of it is the Lord's doing. He gets all the praise and the glory and the honor.

As for the anointing, a definite change comes on me on the platform at these services. I know the presence is with me when I walk on, as it has been in the morning in the hotel and throughout the day. But when I step to the platform it's as though a heavier anointing, or a "thicker mantle," falls.

Before the service, I may pray for a person and

he will fall under the Spirit, but when I move to the platform as a servant of the Lord ready to do battle, there's an awesome presence and power that topples hundreds at a time. It's no longer little Benny Hinn feeling it; it's holy power being displayed — the power of Almighty God.

I actually moved to a new level for me at the miracle crusades as God kept His word with signs and wonders to accompany the preaching of the gospel. I found in a most surprising way that a simple wave of the arm would project power that knocked people to the floor as the anointing touched them. Even a blowing of the breath often caused people to go down like someone being knocked over with a feather. In each of these cases of unusual displays of God's power, I noticed that I felt a certain numbness on my hand. I know the numbness was not the power, but was a result of the power. Neither was the falling of the people the power; it was the evidence of the power.

I was amazed, and more than ever recognized the power of the anointing of the Holy Spirit, which was convincing people of the reality of God in a way I had not experienced before.

Houston Provides Examples

In a crusade in Houston, the Lord saw fit, in a rather impressive way, to show the unusual nature of this waving (or "throwing," as some have called it) and a different type of the "blowing." Gloria Slosser, the wife of a good friend and colleague, having known and served the Father, Son, and Holy Spirit for many years, was sitting in the front row of a crowd of 12,500. She had never been felled by the Spirit, but fully believed in such things.

When the people in front became quite vocal to have me wave or throw at them, I did so, and Gloria, along with about ten rows of people, went down under the power and later said it was a wonderful moment, a happy and laughing moment, as she became keenly aware of the Lord.

A few minutes later, I called several hundred people forward who wanted to make a deep commitment to the Lord and to receive an anointing for it. Gloria was in about the eighth row back. I planned to "throw," but a voice inside me said, "Blow." That's all. "Blow." So I blew into the microphone, and hundreds went down, including Gloria.

She described it later as "something you can't put into words, but it was very good" — also bringing a great awareness of the presence of God. She later made an interesting observation of the two events: "I thought people would go over from the front to the back, and I'd get knocked down in a domino effect. But it wasn't like that. People fell backward from the rear, and you didn't get knocked over. When I fell I landed on a woman behind me, and she soon began to say, 'Get up; get up.' All I could say was 'I can't; I can't.' My knees were too wobbly."

"Also," she said, "I couldn't stop grinning after

that. All the way back to the hotel, I just smiled and smiled. What a delight!"

Some have asked me what I'm trying to do when I throw or blow at them. I only have one answer: "God told me to do it, and I know better than not to obey."

I want to tell you about one other incident in Houston, which has taken place a number of times at other places, but was especially poignant that night. While we were still singing and worshiping, I brought a couple to the platform who had a particular need. As they stood, Steve Brock and I were singing "Name Above All Names," and then the choir joined us on the chorus, which begins so magnificently with "I am Jehovah. I AM that I AM."

At that point, this handsome couple, standing three or four feet from Steve and me, collapsed under the power of the Spirit right there on the platform. No one touched them. God had done it directly without the use of any of His human servants. Why? This couple needed the assurance of the presence of their wonderful Savior. I see evidence like this occurring all over the land as people experience the love and the power of God.

It Happens at Home Too

In my own church, the Orlando Christian Center, we have a great emphasis on teaching and worship, but from time to time, often quite unexpectedly, the Lord will reveal His power spectacularly.

On a recent Sunday evening, I was praying for a number of ministers, and for absolutely no reason, I turned around and saw a lady in a motorized wheelchair. Within me, a voice said, "Go and pray for her — *now!*" It was like a clap — *now!*

I jumped down off the platform — and I'm sure everyone wondered where I was going: "There goes pastor again."

I grabbed the woman and hugged her, tightly, and said, "Release your anointing, Lord."

She jumped up out of the wheelchair. I quickly turned to the choir and yelled, "Lift it up high and praise the Lord!" It was an incredible moment, and when they were slow in getting the music started, I yelled again. That woman was having an amazing miracle, and we needed to praise the Lord. As the intensity of the music arose, the woman got up all alone and began to run around the front of the sanctuary. The place went wild with praise.

It turned out that the woman had had multiple sclerosis, and she told me later with her husband, who just stood and cried like a baby, that she had asked the Lord, "Please do it tonight because we're going home and I may never be able to come back. Please let him come down and pray for me."

The voice of God just said, "Go and pray for her — *now!*"

Amazing. He knows how to get your attention.

Chapter 10

It Didn't Begin Yesterday

The psalmist wrote, "My horn You have exalted like a wild ox; / I have been anointed with fresh oil" (92:10). Similarly the author of Ecclesiastes urged that "your head lack no oil" (9:8). Since He is the third person of the Trinity, the Spirit has never been absent from the mighty acts of God in history. Both of these verses, of course, point to the anointing of the Holy Spirit, since oil is a type of Him in biblical writings.

It would help you to recognize and understand the anointing of the Spirit in our own times if you looked at several personalities from the past.

David, for example, had three anointings, the first taking place when Samuel, the judge and prophet, went to see Jesse and his sons in Bethlehem (1 Sam. 16). You will recall that Samuel said in effect, "Show me your boys, Jesse." After looking at seven of them, he said, "The Lord has not chosen any of these; have you any more?" So Jesse sent for the youngest, who was tending sheep.

112

When David arrived, the Lord said to Samuel, "Anoint him, for this is the one."

That was the first anointing. The second came many years later, when David was anointed in Hebron as king over Judah (2 Sam. 2:4). Seven and a half years later, he was anointed king over Israel (2 Sam. 5:3).

David's first anointing, although directed by God, did not take him beyond slave status with King Saul. His duties included playing the harp to keep the torment of demons from Saul. The second one was followed by ugly conflict with the house of Saul after the king's death.

Only after the third did David receive dominion and authority over all of Israel. Then he left his headquarters at Hebron, took Mount Zion, and established rule over all Zion.

The point for believers is just this: We will never reach the level of dominion and authority that God intends for us until we receive the third anointing — the kingly anointing.

In the same way, the apostles experienced three anointings. The first came when Jesus breathed on them and said, "Receive the Holy Spirit" (John 20:22). The second came when the Holy Spirit fell upon them on the day of Pentecost (Acts 2).

But an even greater anointing came as the power of the early church mounted dramatically. You see, a significant event in chapter four of Acts is often mistaken as simply a repetition of the day of Pentecost, but it is not. It marks an increase in the miraculous power of the apostles' witness to the resurrection of Jesus Christ. Note Acts 4:31, following the disciples' commitment to obey God and not men:

And when they had prayed, the place where they were assembled together was shaken; and they were all filled with the Holy Spirit, and they spoke the word of God with boldness.

The elders of Israel had threatened the apostles and said, "Preach in Christ's name, and you'll be in jail." The apostles stood their ground, and God sent a heavier anointing that produced a supernatural manifestation with the power to reach the world. The place shook, they spoke with boldness, and multitudes were added.

And then comes Acts 5:12-14, which tells us that "through the hands of the apostles many signs and wonders were done among the people . . . and believers were increasingly added to the Lord, multitudes of both men and women."

As for Peter, the anointing was so strong on him that people were healed when he passed by and his shadow fell on them (5:15).

Yes, the third anointing brought greater power in the lives of the apostles and the addition of many, many souls to the Kingdom. That is exactly what we need today so the world can be saved.

A Gold Mine of Teaching

In addition to these examples, the book of Acts, which could just as well be called the Acts of the Holy Spirit, offers a mine of information about the anointing, depending on where you want to concentrate.

For example, *the Holy Spirit announces his entrance.*

You will find this early in Acts. First, Jesus ministered to the apostles through the Holy Spirit, explaining many things (Acts 1:2-3). He promised them power through the Spirit (1:5-8). And then, the Spirit came, letting the whole world know it: "And suddenly there came a sound from heaven, as of a rushing mighty wind, and it filled the whole house where they were sitting." Powerful things then happened. Flames of fire appeared on each of them, they began to speak with other tongues, and they went down into the streets to proclaim the wonderful works of God to people from all over the known world (2:2-11).

The Holy Spirit is gentle, yes; He is comforting, yes; but He also lets you know when He arrives.

Second, *He always brings a burden for lost souls.*

Preaching to the multitudes, Peter, a coward who had failed his Master a few weeks earlier, said:

"Repent, and let everyone of you be baptized in the name of Jesus Christ for the remission

of sins; and you shall receive the gift of the Holy Spirit. For the promise is to you and to your children, and to all who are afar off, as many as the Lord our God will call." And with many other words he testified and exhorted them, saying, "Be saved from this perverse generation." Then those who gladly received his word were baptized; and that day about three thousand souls were added to them. (2:38-41)

No one can prove to me that the Holy Spirit is in his life if he doesn't have a burden to see someone come to Jesus Christ. "You shall receive power and you shall be witnesses," said the Lord. The Spirit is not given to us so we can have spiritual picnics; He's given so we can tell people about Christ.

The next result we find in Acts is *complete unity.*

I seriously question anyone who says he has the Holy Spirit and is always by himself, thinking he's got it all and needs no one else. A clear example of the correct attitude is found in the recorded history of the early church, wherein the converts "continued steadfastly in the apostles' doctrine and fellowship, in the breaking of bread, and in prayers." They were together and held all things in common; "they ate their food with gladness and simplicity of heart." The Lord "added to the church daily" (2:42-47). Lone rangers were not in evidence.

Another thing you will learn is that *the Holy Spirit will flow out of you miraculously to someone else.*

116

Chapter three of Acts makes the point well. It shows Peter and John going up to the temple to pray when they came upon a lame man asking for alms. Peter fixed his eyes upon the man. I love that description. He *fixed* his eyes upon him. What a penetrating look that must have been. "Look at us," he commanded. "So he gave them his attention," it says. "Then Peter said, 'Silver and gold I do not have, but what I do have I give you: In the name of Jesus Christ of Nazareth, rise up and walk.' " What Peter had flowed through him to a needy man. He took him by the hand, lifted him up, and he was healed.

What a story! The Holy Spirit is not given to us simply for our pleasure. He comes to enable us to witness for Christ in power.

Later in History

Moving closer to our times, we find extraordinary acts of the Holy Spirit in people just like you and me.

There was Jonathan Edwards, the eighteenth-century American preacher and theologian. A preacher of virtually no emotion, he would stand behind the pulpit and read his sermons through his thick glasses, seldom looking up at the people. They, meanwhile, would come under great conviction through his messages. One sermon — "Sinners in the Hands of an Angry God" — reportedly brought cries for mercy among the congregation. Some of the people collapsed under the power of

God as he read. That particular message ignited a revival that swept through the colonies with life-changing power. Only the Holy Spirit could have produced such power.

Similarly D.L. Moody, not known for a charismatic speaking style and capable of making numerous speaking mistakes, shook many states and nations with his strong messages that were obviously undergirded by the Spirit of God.

And Charles Finney, instrumental in lighting the revival fires in America, carried such an anointing that his very presence would bring a cloud of glory over a whole area of a city when he spoke. God's glory would be felt inside and outside of meeting halls. People would fall under the power of God, weeping and begging for mercy. Often passersby, most with no interest in God, would crumble under the power and confess their sins.

What brought results like this? It certainly was not oratorial skill or gimmickry.

Kathryn Kuhlman received many snickers from people visiting her meetings for the first time as she glided into the hall in her classy shoes and flowing gowns.

"What a show!" they whispered. But the second she said, "Father," massive auditoriums would come alive with God's presence and power. People would collapse, hundreds would be healed of serious afflictions, and salvation would flow.

It certainly was not gimmickry.

In England, there were the Jeffrey brothers. Few people were familiar with their names, but their anointing was so heavy that they would enter a building, stand behind the pulpit, and say very simply, "The Master is here," and the miracles would occur. Reliable reports were that the lame, the blind, the deaf, and even people missing certain limbs would experience incredible miracles. Reinhard Bonnke, the powerful evangelist who has been transforming much of Africa, believes much of the work of the Spirit in his life can be traced to a prayer spoken over him by one of the Jeffrey brothers many years ago.

Also in England was the marvelous Smith Wigglesworth, with whom my wife's grandmother Lilian worked. One of the most unusual stories I heard from Lil was when a man in the audience died. "Pick him up!" Wigglesworth said. Then he punched the dead man in the stomach, the story goes, and said sternly, "In Jesus' name, rise!" But the man was still dead.

"Pick him up again!" he commanded, even more sternly. "I said in Jesus' name, rise!"

Nothing happened. "Let him go." Still the man was dead and fell to the floor, and for the third time he directed that the man be picked up. "I said in Jesus' name, rise!" And this time, Lil said, he slapped the man in the face. And this time, the man opened his eyes; he was alive!

You may not approve of such struggles, but I trust the point is clear. The powerful manifestation of God's Spirit among His people is not something new. It has been going on since the beginning. And, don't forget, it is for you too!

Chapter 11

Jesus, the I AM

The Holy Spirit is the wonderful Comforter, the Counselor, the Helper, the one sent by the Father and the Son to be with, in, and upon the people of God when Jesus ascended to heaven. And this glorious third person of the Trinity has the primary purpose of revealing the Lord Jesus Christ. As the Spirit of Truth, He has taken the things of Jesus and reveals them to those who will listen, see, and follow.

As I write about the presence and the anointing of the Holy Spirit, you must never lose sight of the Lord Jesus. All is given that you might know, love, and serve Him. So I want to take time at this point to ponder who Jesus is, so that you might better understand the vast importance of this book's subject.

As the songwriter related in this old chorus, *The Lord of Glory:*

He is the Lord of Glory; He is the great
  I AM,

The Alpha and Omega, the beginning and
  the end.
His name is Wonderful, the Prince of
  Peace,
The Everlasting Father, through all eternity.

He is the fullest revelation of God. The Beginning and the End. The First and the Last. The cause and the completion. The Amen.

"I am life eternal," He said. From everlasting to everlasting — Jesus.

You ask, "Lord, what will we see in heaven?"

"I will be your focus."

"What will we do in heaven?"

"Worship and enjoy Me forever."

"What will we hear in heaven?"

"All I reveal to you."

"What is heaven?"

"My creation for you."

Jesus is the center of all. Only He is the "I AM WHO I AM." That's what living and being "in Christ" involves. Once you're saved, you're in Him for good. You're clothed with His life. You're clothed with the Beginning and the End, the Alpha and the Omega.

For a long time, I could not understand how God could say something and it be forever settled. But that's what the Bible says, "Forever, O Lord, your word is settled in heaven" (Ps. 119:89). He speaks it and it's over. Time doesn't affect it; it is eternal.

Jesus *is* the Word. What He says is true.

Without Him, history has no meaning; indeed, there is no history without Him. There is no cause; there is no conclusion.

The whole world asks, "Who am I? Why am I here? Where am I going?" Who, why, where — He's the answer to all three.

Great Meaning

You see, the declaration that "He's the great I AM" has meaning. Remember? Moses asked, "What is Your name?" Who answered? The angel of the Lord, Jesus. "I AM," He said.

Who? "I AM."

Paul, writing about Jesus in Colossians 1:16-17, said:

For by Him all things were created that are in heaven and that are on earth, visible and invisible, whether thrones or dominions or principalities or powers. All things were created through Him and for Him. And He is before all things, and in Him all things consist.

Because of that Moses could say, "Go forward through the sea," and the sea divided. Can't you hear him? "How'd He do that?" The I AM spoke. "Go forward," and Moses stretched out His rod, and the sea parted — not because of the rod, but because of the I AM.

Elijah spoke similarly, and fire fell from heaven. The I AM spoke.

One day a young woman in Nazareth, not knowing what was about to happen, saw an angel who said, in effect, "Mary, the Word of God is about to be a baby in your belly."

"How can this be? Please explain."

"I can't explain it fully."

"Help me to understand."

"I can't."

No one understands. Words are too limited to explain infinity. All you can know — and it's from this side of the event — is that the Limitless One chose to limit Himself to a body. In Mary's belly, eternity was to become flesh. He would come out of her body and she would hold a baby called Jesus in her arms. And Jesus wasn't His full name, for it only meant "Savior" or "Salvation," whereas He was also I AM.

We have been given the name "Jesus" by which to call the "I AM," and Jesus truly is the name above every name. But the question is: What was He called before He became flesh? He was called the Beginning and the End, the Alpha and the Omega, and before that, the I AM.

And He walked this earth.

Holding Everything Together

Every time you move your arm, you are saying, "Jesus is alive." You can't move it without the energy He created. He's the power that keeps your heart pumping. He's the force that keeps your flesh alive.

Think of it, Paul says Jesus the I AM is the power that holds atoms together. Should He step back, the world, including your arm and your heart, would blow to smithereens. Look at Hebrews 1:3: This Son of God holds all things up by the word of His power.

Scientists report that a force keeps bodies and all of nature together. You can tell them what His name is.

Please hear the magnitude of what we're saying: Someone created this marvelous planet called earth, and then that Someone came down and walked on it. He is big enough to create this speck of dust in the vast universe of His creation and then hold it together while He walks on it.

And if that's not enough, think of yourself as a speck of dust on that other speck of dust (earth), and then this limitless Creator of everything decides to live in you. And He has chosen to save you too.

Why?

I AM.

So this One came to earth and when the leaders of the nation He had chosen to live among got angry and said, "We're sons of Abraham," He replied softly, "Before Abraham was, I AM."

"Blasphemy!" they shouted.

"No, I AM."

"How can you be I AM when you're only thirty years old?"

"I AM."

And they crucified Him. But they didn't know

death couldn't hold Him because He is holding death. Nor did they know a grave couldn't hold Him because He is holding the grave.

So He rose from the dead and still said, "I AM."

An Interesting Thought About Man

The Bible says that, after making heaven and earth and their contents, God says, "Let Us make man in Our image," and He even gives him dominion. But He does not give this wonderful creation eternal life with Him. He gives him a choice.

In essence, God says, speaking within the Godhead, "Let's make man to be Our partner; not one with Us, but a partner; not a fourth in the Godhead, but a partner. And let's give him the world We have created, and let's give him a choice whether he'd like life or death."

So God creates Adam, puts him in a Garden, and plants two trees — one the Tree of Life, the other the Tree of Death, which was also called the Tree of the Knowledge of Good and Evil. And God waits to see what Adam will do.

Now no place in the book of Genesis does God reveal Himself to Adam. Think of it. God creates a man, but never tells him who He the Creator is. The first person to hear "I AM" is Moses (Exod. 3:14).

Why not Adam? God waits to see Adam's choice regarding life and death. The point is a big one. You will never have the revelation about the I AM unless you choose Him. God will not force

Himself on anyone, not even the first man.

Had Adam chosen the Tree of Life, he would have lived in perfection forever and what a glorious thing that would have been for the human race. Don't forget: God intended for man to multiply before sin entered the picture. It would have been wonderful.

When Adam chooses the Tree of the Knowledge of Good and Evil he dies, and when he experiences it he doesn't like it. He must have tried to get to the Tree of Life, for God sends an angel to block him.

Think of that Tree of Life as Jesus Christ. Had Adam taken of the tree at the very beginning, he would have entered into unceasing revelation of the Word of the Living God. But he chose the other tree.

Why Jesus Came to Earth

I remember Billy Graham's likening God and man's situation after the fall to one in which you, a human being, created this little creature called an ant. And being its creator, you loved the little ant and took care of it. One day you saw the ant heading toward death, so what were you to do? How were you to tell it that it was going to die?

The problems were overwhelming. One, the ant doesn't think as you think. Two, it can't hear you. Three, it can't see you. Four, it can't understand you. If you try to touch it, you may kill it. If you put your hand in front of it, it will climb over your hand and keep going. What are you to do?

The only thing to do was become an ant and say, "Don't go that way; you're going to die. Follow me."

When we think of the Lord Jesus, we must try to understand that He is far more than the limited man the world has seen with natural eyes — even the miracle-working man. Think about Him as only a man and you haven't begun to fathom the limitless Being He is. Yes, He said He was "the door," but what's behind the door? That's the exciting question, and you and I have much of that still ahead of us.

But the Lord, over the centuries, has been revealing His person, a little at a time through various men. The beginning of the letter to the Hebrews speaks of it:

God, who at various times and in different ways spoke in time past to the fathers by the prophets, has in these last days spoken to us by His Son, whom He has appointed heir of all things, through whom also He made the worlds; who being the brightness of His glory and the express image of His person, and upholding all things by the word of His power, when He had by Himself purged our sins, sat down at the right hand of the Majesty on high.

At first God revealed Himself one drop at a time through the mouths of men. Each had one revelation, one word, one sermon, if you will: Enoch, Noah, Abraham, Isaac, Jacob, Joseph, Moses, Joshua, Caleb, Gideon, David, Solomon, right down to John the Baptist.

But one day God said, in effect, "Let's no longer speak through someone else's mouth. Let's become visible and speak." So "the Word became flesh and dwelt among us" (John 1:14).

We had the limitless revelation we call Jesus, although we still could not see this revelation with our natural minds. But Paul teaches us that we have received "the Spirit who is from God, that we might know the things that have been freely given to us by God." But, he adds, "The natural man does not receive the things of the Spirit of God . . . because they are spiritually discerned . . . but we have the mind of Christ" (1 Cor. 2:12-16).

That is astounding!

As you walk with the Spirit, living in His presence, anointed with His power, you will find yourself understanding more and more of this limitless Lord and Savior, the great I AM. You will receive one touch, and you will cry, "Touch me again." You will not be satisfied with yesterday's touch, and you will find yourself all the time saying, "One more time; please, just one more time." Every revelation will make you hungry for another.

You may find yourself asking, "Will I ever come to the end of Your revelation?" And He will say, "Never!" One revelation is just the beginning of the next. And I want to show you how to get on with this walk and to keep on it.

Chapter 12

It's for You — Now

So many people want the power of God, but fail to understand that it will not come until they first experience His presence. And when the presence comes, the first evidence will be the manifestation of the fruit of the Spirit, as I said earlier. The fruit will be evident in everyday contacts with those around you. And when the fruit is genuinely there, the Lord will anoint you with His Spirit, which is power.

It goes like this: The presence of God is the vehicle that brings the power. Power follows the presence, not the other way around. The presence and the fruit come together. The anointing and the power do too.

When you receive the anointing of the Spirit, the result is the fulfillment of Acts 1:8: "You shall be witnesses to Me." This means that speaking in tongues or manifesting any gifts of the Spirit without the presence is not what God was talking about. You must have the presence first, which will give you the fruit, and this will invite God to dwell within you. Then the anointing will come, which means power. And you will be His witness.

God spoke clearly to me about this: "I don't anoint vessels that are empty of me. I anoint vessels that are *full of Me*." This was a revelation. We receive the baptism of the Holy Spirit — being immersed in Him, filled to overflowing, indwelt. The experience is real, not merely emotion and goose bumps. Then the fruit of the Spirit should pour out of our lives, touching those around us.

When that occurs, the Lord will anoint us as we walk with and obey Him, and at that point the power begins — the power to serve Him. Then we can boldly inherit the promises of God to see the unbeliever's heart soften and turn toward God and to see the signs and wonders like those recorded in the book of Acts.

Your Countenance Will Shine

You will recall that when Moses saw the glory and presence of God at Mount Sinai he descended with his face shining like a light. People could not even look at his face. When you, too, have an encounter with the presence of God, it will be obvious. It may even show on your face and certainly will show in your conduct. Your countenance will announce to those around you, "I am different. I have been in the presence of God Almighty."

Whereas you once were self-conscious, with little or no God-consciousness — and manifesting only yourself — you will lose self-consciousness, gain God-consciousness, and manifest the fruit of God.

Adam provides a good illustration. When he lost God-consciousness and was stripped of the presence and glory that had clothed him, he was filled with his own self-consciousness. Then he said, "I was afraid." At that point he began to hide from God, his Friend, the Creator of heaven and earth.

Fear is the first result of self-consciousness, and boldness is the first result of God-consciousness. When we become God-conscious, we are no longer forced to trust in ourselves and our own strength, but God's presence resides within, bringing power and authority to our lives. We no longer must fight our battles in our own strength, but we can boldly call upon God Almighty through the authority of the Spirit.

I trust you understand. The presence of the Spirit will indwell your spirit, while the anointing of the Spirit will cover and saturate you. You must have both to adequately show forth Jesus to the world to be His witness. It takes the presence to change you, while it takes the anointing to communicate the presence out of you.

There Is Only One Way

"So," you say, "what am I to do?"

There is only one way. Prayer. That means war, all-out war. It is primarily war against the self, which is the biggest enemy. If you can't lose sight of self, you'll not know the presence of God.

The flesh dies in prayer. And you will have to battle to achieve that. Most of you will find, just as I did, that when you first go into real prayer, all you think about are your desperate sins and needs. All you can say is "forgive *me*, have mercy on *me*, help *me*, lead *me*," and so on. It's all me, me, me.

Now don't misunderstand me. You must confess your sins, ask for and receive forgiveness, and seek guidance, but you need to get on with communing with the Lord, listening to and talking about the things that are on His heart. You need to love Him and thank Him and worship Him. That is the fruit of His presence. The other things will come in His time, not yours.

Five minutes in the presence of God, in fellowship with Him, are worth a year in the me-me-me mode. And you will find that as you gain victory in this war, you will begin to experience the presence. Your pleasure will be so great that you will gladly give up the flesh and the self simply to bask in His presence.

God will talk to you; you will talk to Him. He will share so much with you and tell you so much. You will delight ecstatically in His love and warmth, His tenderness, His wisdom. From this you will move into obedience to his voice, and that is the key to the anointing of the Holy Spirit.

He will entrust you with little things, to determine your faithfulness, how you will obey. If you are faithful in a little, He will entrust you with more . . . and more . . . and more. His power will be upon you to fulfill the calling He has made upon you.

The Power Is for All

Let me say a word about calling. The anointing of the Holy Spirit is for every Christian, and, as I said in describing the leper's anointing in Chapter 9, everyone who has been born again has received the initial anointing of the Spirit, which I've called the leper's.

The anointing beyond that will match your calling as a Christian. Some are called to direct service of the Lord — preachers, evangelists, healing evangelists, pastors, teachers. Others may be writers, musicians, administrators, helpers, group leaders, hospitality providers, whatever. Others may be spouses, parents, general schoolteachers, business people, carpenters, laborers, and so on.

Assuming that by calling and intent they are all serving the Lord — in the church or "secularly" — each can and should receive the anointing to fit the calling.

In much of this book I have been using language that speaks more pointedly to the anointing of the Holy Spirit for direct ministerial calling, if you will. That accounts for much of the discussion of attacking the devil and sickness and ministering directly from the pulpit or platform to God's people as God's servant. This should not diminish by the tiniest fraction your eagerness for the anointing in whatever you're doing.

Eventually — the sooner, the better — you should get to the place where you are praying without ceasing. It becomes your life, for you do it long enough and your nature changes. Your lifestyle changes.

Certainly you must live a natural life; we all do. Jesus, although rising early and going off by Himself a lot, wasn't on His knees twenty-four hours a day. None of us can do that. There's regular work to be done, children to attend, and such.

Some of the most precious times I've ever had came in ordinary living situations. I think of my own children and the wonderful times we have had talking and praying together. I'm not off in my room or out in the woods alone. I'm right there with the children and my wife and experiencing the same beautiful presence of the Lord. It's a totally different kind of anointing, just the tender presence of God and the blessing of our family life. It's not the anointing and power for a healing service. But it's very important, and very real.

I've had the same thing talking to my staff at the Orlando Christian Center — encouraging, sympathizing, exhorting, chastising. The presence is very real as I simply say, "Jesus."

But the point is, Jesus was in continual fellowship with His Father, and we should be in continual fellowship with Him, too, by way of the wonderful Holy Spirit.

Quiet times, as I've said, give birth to this praying without ceasing, and we must not neglect them.

People always ask me about my own private prayer times. I understand their desire for instruction, and modeling is often the best kind of instruction. But, really, prayer is so private, so precious, so intimate that I ask people not to get hung up on the way I do it, but rather to let God show them how they are to do it.

There are times when I begin to pray, all alone with the Lord in my room or outdoors or wherever, as long as it is private and quiet, and I will get caught up in such a way that I will go for half a day or more. Then there are times when I may be alone with Him for only an hour.

I've had times of traveling overseas when, because of schedules or interferences, I won't have more than five minutes. But, remember, the Lord trained me in continual fellowship many years ago, and I never, never neglect that.

And on some of those days of interruptions and trials, I've gone on the platform in a healing service so anointed that one would have thought I'd been praying and reading the Bible all day.

Don't Forget the Bible

As for the Bible, it is an essential part of prayer time. I don't begin a day without getting into the Scripture, even before praying. I must do it. It's God's Word, and I must have it pouring into me over my soul — and so must you.

Furthermore, when you pray and experience the

presence of God, you should have the Bible at your side. He will take you to passages, and He will teach you. And when you are troubled over a passage, ask Him about it. He will teach you. The Bible says very plainly that He's your Teacher — indeed, the Spirit is the only Teacher you need.

Remember 1 John 2:27:

> *But the anointing which you have received from Him abides in you, and you do not need that anyone teach you; but as the same anointing teaches you concerning all things, and is true, and is not a lie, and just as it has taught you, you will abide in Him.*

As you pursue this wonderful course of life, you will discover principles and doctrines in the Bible that are of first importance, and I truly do mean first, as you will see.

Chapter 13

Two Profound Basics

As you proceed toward your anointing of the Holy Spirit, dear Christian, I want to discuss two basic doctrines that are so profound as to shake the entire planet, indeed the entire universe. They address repentance and the blood of Christ, which, of course, go hand in glove.

Repentance is the first step toward receiving the anointing, no matter what the level at which you stand.

Now, I can hear the voices of protest: "But I've repented; I'm born again!"

To the fact that you're born again, I say, "Hallelujah!" To the thought that repentance is therefore behind you and no longer an issue, I say, "No way!"

Let me begin by calling up Acts 2:38, which follows Peter's remarkable sermon to the unbelievers in Jerusalem on the day of Pentecost. The power of the Holy Spirit had fallen on one hundred and twenty Jesus-followers and this miracle was being manifested in various ways, especially in the empowerment of Peter's preaching.

The Bible says that the listeners were "cut to the heart" by the message and asked, "What can we do?" Peter replied:

Repent, and let every one of you be baptized in the name of Jesus Christ for the remission of sins; and you shall receive the gift of the Holy Spirit. For the promise is to you and to your children, and to all who are afar off, as many as the Lord our God will call.

"Repent and be baptized," he said. Now look at the verse that has been so pivotal in my teaching about the anointing of the Holy Spirit: "Ye shall receive power, after that the Holy Ghost is come upon you: and ye shall be witnesses unto me . . . unto the uttermost part of the earth" (Acts 1:8 KJV).

So we have the promise of power after the coming of the Spirit upon us. Spirit. Anointing. Power. And they come after repentance.

And what's it for? To be "witnesses unto Me." That's important. You receive the power to tell people about Jesus Christ. You will not tell the world what you are like, how great you have become, what a miserable sinner you were. No, you will tell them about your great High Priest, about your great King, about your wonderful Savior whose name is Jesus. You will tell what He can do with a life that's empty.

138

I can hear the rumbles again: "What do you mean? Isn't the power given so I can tell my experiences, my testimony?"

No, the Holy Spirit does not glorify what you have been through. He brings Jesus to the center. He shows the world what Jesus has gone through to get You to heaven, not what you have gone through to get there. "You shall be witnesses to *me*" — to who *Jesus* is, what *Jesus* has done, what *Jesus* has said, what *Jesus* has promised.

I have made all the crazy mistakes, beloved. I do not speak only about others. Before my encounter with real life and real power in Pittsburgh eighteen years ago, I attended churches that were so noisy and wild that they obviously thought noise was power. Everybody had a tambourine. They apparently thought tambourines brought the Holy Ghost. All I found was that I was dying on the vine; I had no life within me. I would stand in church and squeeze the back of the pew so hard that the blood would stop flowing in my fingers. Every Sunday I would go to the altar and weep and beg God for the power that I saw promised in the Bible. I had everybody who had anything laying hands on me. I'd stay in my room, playing the tambourine and trying every formula, reading every book and hearing every broadcast.

I knew the promises of power, and I knew they had to be mine. Today I know they're not only mine, but also my children's.

And the key is repentance. It puts you on the

road to great fire and you will reach the destination God intends.

What Does It Mean?

So what does repentance mean? Let's start with what it doesn't mean. It doesn't mean to go to the altar, shed a few tears, say, "I'm sorry, Lord," and go out to do the same thing.

Repentance is a daily experience. And it's a supernatural experience, not something you can humanly accomplish by yourself. It's a gift of the Holy Spirit. Repentance rests on "whoever confesses and forsakes them [his sins] will have mercy" (Prov. 28:13). That's the true meaning — not only confessing, but also forsaking.

Have nothing to do with it any more. You get on your knees and you say, "Lord, never again," and you don't walk out until the thing is dealt with.

Until it is dealt with, you will not receive the Holy Spirit, and you will dry on the vine. There are far too many Christians sitting in their sanctuaries, dying on the vine for lack of life and power. They say, "But I've got faith." Faith? When the gift of God comes — the Spirit — He will give life to that faith.

Furthermore, this matter of faith has been talked about, misunderstood, and abused for far too long. People have cried for faith, faith, faith until they've blown it to pieces. They have so misused and misinterpreted the doctrine that they have completely messed themselves up — and thousands of others too. Faith, as I've just said, is a gift from God, gladly given and kept alive by the Spirit.

As for repentance, which is the first step to the anointing of the Holy Spirit, it must occur in every sinful action of your life, even in simple things — such as repenting if you haven't prayed, repenting if you haven't read the Word, repenting if you have neglected the Lord, repenting if you have lightly treated the awesome gift of the presence on your life, repenting if you have removed Jesus from your conversation.

Any of these sins show you are empty and dead, or at least on the way there. They disappoint the only One who counts. And there are much worse ones, which you know as well as I. They're more direct, often gross, sometimes vile. And naturally they must be dealt with, and quickly.

How do you do it? You go to God and you say, "Lord, give me a repentant heart." Like David, you say, "Create in me a clean heart, O God." You say, "The sacrifices of God are a broken spirit, a broken and a contrite heart." You say, "Forgive me, Lord, for seeking the things of this world." You say, "Forgive me, Lord, for leaving my first love." You say, "Forgive me, Lord, for being so lukewarm." You say, "Take not Your Holy Spirit from me."

You must receive the power of the Spirit daily to battle with the flesh in repentance. For it is a daily battle: "No, no, no, no" to the enemy; "yes, yes, yes, yes" to God.

Good friends, we must say to the church — to ourselves — "Get back, get back to repentance with a true heart." We must start living the kind of life that is crucified with Christ daily, for if we do, we won't be able to keep the Holy Spirit away. We won't even have to ask Him to fill us.

Now, hear me on one more major point. God does not want His people sitting around crying all the time. That is not repentance. He wants us to be sensitive to our sins, to deal with them immediately, and to get on with lives of joy in the power of God.

Repentance. Presence. Anointing. Service. Joy.

What Makes It Work?

As you move toward your anointing of the Holy Spirit, I want to write briefly about a fact that stands behind everything we're talking about, especially the first step of repentance.

In the Bible, pointing toward the first coming of the Messiah, the prophet Zechariah says: "As for you also, because of the blood of your covenant, I will set your prisoners free from the waterless pit" (Zech. 9:11).

God, talking about His people, is saying that the blood of Christ, the blood of the new covenant, will set them free. And the sad fact is that many people have no clue as to how they can and should apply the blood to their lives and receive the liberty of repentance and all the truths of the faith.

Many are still bound. Demons harass them. Sickness has hit them and their children. Confusion is destroying their peace.

It should not be so. The Bible teaches us that the shed blood of Jesus Christ causes six things to occur in our lives in opposition to the turmoil striking so much of the church:

- Ephesians 1:7 says, "In Him we have redemption through His blood." We are redeemed by His blood. Redeemed from what? From the kingdom of darkness, the kingdom of Satan, who for now is allowed to rule the world. Christ knowingly "shed" His blood, not accidentally "spilled" it, and redeemed (a marketplace word) us.

  You can look Satan in the eye and tell him he has no control over you, for you were legally bought back. You see, God and Satan both know you were legally bought back, but do you know it? When attacked by the enemy, you do not need to cry out, "Oh, God, help me!" You can legally say, "Devil, get your filthy hands off me."

- Ephesians 1:7 goes on to say, "[In Him we have through His blood] the forgiveness of sins . . ." We were forgiven by the blood of Christ. Now forgiveness does not deal with buying back anything, but it deals with what you did as a sinner. God redeems you and then forgets everything you did, which means looking at you and saying you never did anything

143

wrong. He forgets your "sins," which are the things you thought about, and your "iniquities," which are the acts of the thoughts.

In fact, Isaiah 38:17 speaks of God's casting all our sins behind His back. And when God throws, they keep flying forever.

- First John 1:7 says, if we walk in the light, "the blood of Jesus Christ . . . cleanses us from all sin." Please note the present tense of the action: cleanses. It is a now experience. Forgiveness deals with what you did; cleansing deals with what you're doing.

  Think of it. The blood of Christ redeems and saves you at a point in time, forgives everything you've done in past years, hours, and minutes; and cleanses your very thoughts and acts right now. If you repent, bingo, the thing you're thinking that instant is cleansed. There is tremendous power in the blood.

- Romans 5:9 says, "Having now been justified by His blood, we shall be saved from wrath through Him." Justification, which has been accomplished by His blood, deals with your future — the wrath, which is to come. It's a startling statement, but if you're justified, anything you will do from now on is taken care of.

  Obviously, that needs explanation, since someone by now is already saying, "Well now, if I'm justified I can go sin tomorrow and God will take care of it. Why not live it up, etc., etc.?" The fact is, if you *decide*

144

knowingly and willingly — that's the pivotal phrase — if you decide knowingly and willingly to sin, your justification flies out the window. Willful sinning, knowingly and intentionally, is not of God. There is no more place for repentance. Simply said, your continued justification is dependent upon obedience, and obedience, you will remember, is the way to the anointing. Sin committed in weakness or ignorance or by accident is not the same as the former.

• Colossians 1:20 says, "And by Him to reconcile all things to Himself . . . having made peace through the blood of His cross." God has reconciled you to Himself and there is peace between Him and you. He has brought you back and restored fellowship with the Father, Son, and Holy Spirit. In its fullest sense, reconciliation here means "one with God."

You may say, "I sure don't see it." Be patient. The Bible says we're being changed from glory to glory; you'll get there. For now you're there by faith, but you'll get there by experience. And faith is substance.

• First Peter 1:2 says: "[To the pilgrims,] elect according to foreknowledge of God the Father, in sanctification of the Spirit, for obedience and sprinkling of the blood of Jesus Christ." As hard as it may be to fathom, the Bible says you have been sanctified by the blood.

145

Now sanctification is tied directly to the anointing. The anointing will not come without sanctification, for *sanctification* means "set apart."

Recall the account in Leviticus 14 of the leper who stays outside the camp. It says the priest goes outside the camp, takes the blood, dips hyssop in the blood, sprinkles the leper seven times, and the leper is cleansed from leprosy. After this, the leper comes into the camp, and the priest takes blood, the same blood he sprinkled him with earlier, and applies it to the cleansed leper's ear, thumb, and toe. Now this is important: ear, thought life; thumb, work life; and toe, everyday walk life. The priest then puts the oil on his ear, thumb, and toe and pours a handful over the cleansed leper's head. This is the fullness of the anointing: thought life, work life, and walk life.

The significance of this is that so many of us, even after we're cleansed and inside the camp, don't recognize the extra protection that is ours for all of life, not simply "church life." The devil can and does hit our thought life, our work life, and our daily walk through life. I, for example, apply the blood on my wife, children, home, cars, everything.

The blood on these aspects of life, if applied, protects them. The oil sanctifies them.

Now hear me on this: The blood precedes the oil. The Lord will never anoint you with the Holy Spirit until you apply the blood to your life — all of your life.

A great evangelist named Mary Woodworth Etter would apply the blood on an entire congregation, and the power of God would fall in a miraculous way. The Spirit answers the blood.

Just Do It

How do you and I cover ourselves with the blood? Romans 3:25 (KJV) gives us three keys: "[Christ Jesus,] whom God hath set forth to be a propitiation through faith in His blood, to declare His righteousness for the remission of sins that are past, through the forbearance of God."

The first key is *knowledge*. We must know what the blood has done. No one can apply it if he is ignorant about it. We must study it, learn it, know it. What did the blood do, and what will it now do?

The second key is *faith in what we know*. Let faith arise in our hearts. How can we apply the blood unless we believe what we are saying?

The third key is *declaration by faith of what we know*. To declare means to speak out loud. If I know it and believe it, then I will speak it — not as though by magic or superstitiously, but by faith in God, who never lies.

It comes out quite simply: "It is written that through the blood of Jesus, I have forgiveness of sins. I am forgiven. It is written that I have been redeemed by the blood of Christ. I have been bought back. It is written that I can apply the blood of Christ to my thought life, my work life, and my everyday walk life. I apply the blood and all of my life is protected."

147

It Touches All There Is

The power of the blood is truly without ending. We find that in just one of the sixty-six books of the Bible the blood of Christ has

- destroyed Satan — Hebrews 2:14
- destroyed the fear of death — Hebrews 2:15
- purged your conscience — Hebrews 9:14
- cleansed heaven — Hebrews 9:23
- given boldness — Hebrews 10:19
- promised perfection — Hebrews 13:20
- guaranteed the second coming — Hebrews 9:28

And now, my friends, you must take steps to maintain and retain the anointing that has or is being given to you, as you will now see.

Chapter 14

The Example of Jesus

In my church, I nudge the people over and over and tell them, "If you want the anointing, tell someone about Jesus." After all, everyone knows we're in a battle for souls with Satan. And battles with the devil require the anointing.

I am convinced that if anyone or any church stops serving — stops essentially telling someone about Jesus — the anointing will leave. After all, it is given for spiritual warfare and God wants us to use it for His glory.

The Lord moved upon me at a recent Wednesday night service with a strong word. The church must go all-out in its witness to the local community and to the world. I promised the people that we would immediately begin a series of teachings for those who needed it, so the whole church could actively make a strong witness to everyone.

That night I noted the wonderful words of Isaiah that open the sixty-first chapter: "The Spirit of the LORD GOD is upon Me."

What powerful words. Jesus used them at the opening of His ministry when He was on earth. Luke's Gospel says the Lord was "full of the Spirit," which surprises many people who don't know that Jesus Christ, who was fully man as well as fully God, had to be filled with the Holy Spirit to battle Satan, just as we do.

In this passage, Jesus had already been anointed by the Spirit while being baptized by John the Baptist and had been tempted by Satan in the wilderness. Then He went to the synagogue in Nazareth, "as His custom was," and stood up to read. He was handed the book of Isaiah, Luke says, and turned to the place where it was written:

The Spirit of the LORD is upon Me,
Because He has anointed Me to preach the
  gospel to the poor.
He has sent Me to heal the brokenhearted,
To preach deliverance to the captives
And recovery of sight to the blind,
To set at liberty those who are oppressed,
To preach the acceptable year of the LORD
  (Luke 4:18-19).

Luke tells us that as Jesus sat down, "The eyes of all in the synagogue were fixed on Him." I love that word *fixed*. They had felt the presence and the power of God in their midst. They were left staring. Then Jesus told them why they had felt the power in a way they hadn't before: "Today this Scripture is fulfilled in your hearing."

"I am that One," Jesus was saying. "I am the One Isaiah was describing." You will recall that throughout His ministry — and even after His resurrection — Jesus spoke of the Scripture's witness to Him. The Old Testament tells in a variety of ways of the coming of the kingdom and the coming of the King. And He spoke often of this witness, as did His apostles later.

It's odd, isn't it, that apparently those same people who had "fixed" their eyes upon Him and "marveled" at Him would soon rise up and try to throw Him over a cliff.

The passage shows us not only that the anointing had come upon the Lord, but also that it had come for more than one reason. It was for (1) preaching the gospel, (2) healing broken hearts, (3) proclaiming deliverance to the captives, (4) working miracles, (5) liberating the oppressed, and (6) preaching the acceptable year of the Lord.

And so it is with us.

First and foremost, if we want the anointing, we are to "preach the gospel to the poor." After all, that's just what the Holy Spirit came upon you for — to be a witness.

Why does it say "the poor"? It's true that Jesus frequently identified with those who lacked adequate money and shelter. But there's more than that: All of us are spiritually poor without the Lord. So we are to preach the gospel, the good news, the glad tidings.

According to Isaiah and Luke, the anointing came also to "heal the brokenhearted." What great, great news for our brokenhearted world! Oh, what the Holy Spirit could do if we were available! All He needs is a yielded vessel. Would you be that vessel today? As you read these pages, ask Him to make you that vessel — now.

Preaching and witnessing without the anointing will do little good for the broken in heart. Think of the men, women, and children you know who are crushed by circumstances that could be healed. Think of the families, the divorcées, the lonely, the fearful, the outcasts, the suicidal, the poverty-stricken, the victims of bigotry. The list goes on and on. Only the anointing will heal all hearts of men and women — that's what the Bible says!

Preaching Deliverance

The Lord Jesus was also anointed "to preach deliverance to the captives." The people were bound, tortured, ravaged by devils.

Modern man laughs, but the need for deliverance is even greater today. Think of the bondage filling our newspapers and television daily, the awful, awful captivity. Alcohol and drugs. Illicit sex and homosexuality. False religions and witchcraft. Ill-gained wealth and materialism.

The Lord Jesus said in Mark 16:17, "In My name they will cast out demons." The Holy Spirit is the only power on earth that can destroy the power of Satan. And He has given you, the believer, that power. We must get going, saints!

Jesus also said He was anointed to preach "recovery of sight to the blind." Blindness is not limited to the physical, but is found in the spiritual realm as well. Jesus is the answer for both.

His list of works, for Himself and for us, also included "to set at liberty those who are oppressed." As with captivity, the awful prevalence of oppression eats at every nation of the world. It will fall only by the power of God.

The ruler of this present darkness is the master of oppression and will be defeated only by the power of God. That, beloved, is why the "witnesses unto Me" must have the anointing of the Holy Spirit, the power of Almighty God.

The last of the works Jesus cited as His, but certainly not the least, was "to preach the acceptable year of the Lord."

This, He proclaimed, is the time — the time of grace.

The Savior of the world has come, bringing salvation to humankind before the coming of the end.

The Times That Lie Ahead

The Bible speaks much about the coming of the end. For our purposes, I want to share with you some of the things that the Holy Spirit showed me will be fulfilled for believers as that time approaches.

The Bible tells us, in Acts 3:19-21, that we should repent,

that your sins may be blotted out, so that

153

times of refreshing may come from the presence of the Lord, and that He may send Jesus
Christ, who was preached to you before, whom
heaven must receive until the times of res-
toration of all things, which God has spoken
by the mouth of all His holy prophets since
the world began.

The Holy Spirit, through Peter, said everything
that had been promised — everything that the
prophets had declared — would come to pass and
be fulfilled before the return of Jesus Christ to earth.

The Spirit of the Lord led me to Isaiah 35 to
show the things that are promised to believers,
the things that are coming upon us very soon. I
want to share this with you now, and please remember that everything written in the Old Covenant is a shadow of what you and I receive in
this dispensation of grace. We are walking in the
substance of what the Old Testament prophets declared. Isaiah 35 begins:

The wilderness and the wasteland shall be
   glad for them,
And the desert shall rejoice and blossom as
   the rose;
It shall blossom abundantly and rejoice,
Even with joy and singing.
The glory of Lebanon shall be given to it,
The excellence of Carmel and Sharon.
They shall see the glory of the LORD, the
   excellency of our God. (v. 1-2)

154

As someone who grew up in Israel, I understand something of what the Bible means when it speaks of wilderness. There you find snakes, scorpions, death, drought. It is symbolic of the believer who is dry, living in that spiritual drought with snakes and so forth. But God promises that the day will come when that dry and empty life will be blessed with God's abundant power. How will life and blessing be given to that dry and empty place?

Isaiah goes on to say that "the glory of Lebanon shall be given to it." I remember that, when I was a child, the winds from Lebanon, the north, would blow every now and then and I could smell the wonderful cedars of Lebanon. These same cedars are what the Bible is talking about when it speaks of the Glory of Lebanon. When Isaiah speaks of their wonderful fragrance, he is foretelling a new atmosphere of God's presence that will change your desert — your spiritual life — into a place of beauty and abundance.

Going on, the prophet then speaks of "the excellence of Carmel and Sharon." The Sharon Valley in Israel today is the most fertile valley in the Middle East, the place of excellent produce and the most beautiful flowers in the region. The same is true of Carmel. In Isaiah this speaks of a fresh revelation of God's Word, telling of the seed that will be planted to bear beautiful fruit.

"They shall see the glory of the LORD," Isaiah then says, "the excellency of our God." He speaks of a new vision of God's glory. And what did we find earlier in chapter seven to be the glory of the Lord? You will recall that Moses asked to see God's glory in Exodus 33:18. Then, in Exodus 34:5–6, what did He see but God's attributes, His personality. In other words, Isaiah speaks of our seeing a new vision of God Himself.

So, putting these together, we see God's intention to provide a new atmosphere around our lives, a new word from heaven, a new revelation from His Word, and a new vision of Himself. When that happens, our wilderness experience of death and drought will be changed into the Promised Land.

There is more, for Isaiah continues in verses 3–4:

> Strengthen the weak hands,
> And make firm the feeble knees.
> Say to those who are fearful-hearted,
> "Be strong, do not fear!
> Behold, your God will come with
>   vengeance,
> With the recompense of God;
> He will come and save you."

There will be worldwide evangelism. Those who were transformed by the new atmosphere, the new revelation, and the new vision of God are now strengthening the weak hands and the feeble knees, and are saying to the world, "Fear not, behold, God is coming to save you!"

Of course, this prophecy was spoken about Israel in the Millenium, but, as a shadow of the substance of New Testament times, it has spiritual application to you and to me. Certainly we look all around us and see wilderness, but God will transform that for us, and we will see unprecedented, worldwide evangelism as we go out to minister to the world.

And what other results did Isaiah say would come from this transformed wilderness? Look at verses 5–6 again: the blind shall see, the deaf shall hear, the lame shall leap, the dumb shall sing!

This is miraculous. The supernatural power of God will be released for physical healing.

This recalls the day years ago when I heard Kathryn Kuhlman prophesy in her own inimitable way that the day would arrive, before the coming of the Lord, when the power of God would be so great that everyone would be healed. "There will not be one sick saint in the body of Christ," she declared.

With her customary drama, pointing of finger, and hand on hip, she asked, "Could it be today?"

Of course, she never saw it come, but it will come. The Holy Spirit has convinced me of that.

We should not be skeptical about God's willingness to move upon His people in that way. We find evidence in the Scripture to support supernatural provision, including healing. In Psalm 105:37, for example, we find these words about the children of Israel when He brought them out of Egypt: "And there was none feeble among His tribes." That is a magnificent state of abiding health. Divine health, not merely divine healing. Permanent healing. I am confident that the day is coming when every believer will be healthy.

Here is a key point: If God would heal all under the Mosaic Law, how much more will He heal under grace? Furthermore, when Jesus healed during His time on earth, He was under the Dispensation of the Law; that being the case, how much more could we be healed under the Dispensation of Grace?

Thus, it is not strange for Isaiah to prophesy that, as our wilderness is changed to beauty, God will minister miraculous healing during a time of worldwide evangelism.

He doesn't stop there, however, as chapter 35 continues with a third result:

For waters shall burst forth in the
  wilderness,
And streams in the desert.
The parched ground shall become a pool,
And the thirsty land springs of water.
  (v. 6-7)

A mighty, new anointing will come upon our wilderness, and rivers of living water will burst — gush — forth from us. This will not be a small thing. It could be like a double portion that will produce streams and pools and springs. It will be a mighty baptism of the Holy Spirit.

The move of the Spirit in those days will come through us. God did not say in Joel 2:28 and Acts 2:17 that He would "pour *down*" but "pour *out*" His Spirit. He will use us.

A fourth result of this transformation is foretold by Isaiah in this manner:

In the habitation of jackals ["dragons,"
  KJV], where each lay,
There shall be grass with reeds and rushes.
  (35:7)

God will deliver His people from every demonic influence. The dragons or jackals — the demons — have been lying in the grass, destroying it, but it will be restored as they are driven out.

Fifth, holiness will come to the body of Christ, as portrayed in these words:

A highway shall be there, and a road,
And it shall be called the Highway of
  Holiness.
The unclean shall not pass over it,
But it shall be for others.
Whoever walks the road, although a fool,
Shall not go astray. (35:8)

The holiness will be so great that it will stabilize even the double-minded. They will quit jumping from one thing to another.

The sixth result will be this:

No lion shall be there,
Nor shall any ravenous beast go up on it;
It shall not be found there,
But the redeemed shall walk there. (35:9)

159

Quite simply, Satan and his demons will be totally absent from the body of Christ.

Finally,

And the ransomed of the LORD shall return,
And come to Zion with singing,
With everlasting joy on their heads.
They shall obtain joy and gladness.
And sorrow and sighing shall flee away.
    (35:10)

I believe this points to the Rapture. For only then — when we are out of this world — can sorrow and sighing flee away.

Greater Works for You

The Bible declares that these things are coming from the Lord, and as we look around us nothing seems more incredible. Yet Jesus said in another portion of the Scripture, "And greater works than these shall [you] do, because I go to My Father" (John 14:12).

It is startling. The Bible is saying that there is one thing Jesus could not do that we can. For years and years this statement baffled me. I thought, *What could be greater than what the Lord did — greater than raising the dead, casting out demons, calming the sea, commanding the wind to stop, and healing the lame, the blind, the deaf, What is greater?*

One day the Holy Spirit revealed something to me that transformed my life. He who could call

Lazarus from the dead and still the waters could not stand and say, "Look at me, a sinner saved by the grace of God. I once was lost, but now am found, blind but now I see, bound but now I'm free."

Sin never touched the spotless Son of the living God. He is the only One who lived a perfect life.

So today you and I can stand before this dark world and say, "Look at me and see what Jesus has done." The new anointing that is coming upon us in the transformation of our wilderness, as Isaiah revealed, will allow us to be witnesses for Him, and the greater work will be done in an unprecedented way.

Think about it. The day is coming when the anointing of the Holy Spirit will be so great upon us that we are going to see worldwide evangelism, a worldwide release of the supernatural, a fresh anointing of power, deliverance from every demonic influence in the body of Christ, holiness throughout the church, total absence of Satan among believers, the coming of the Lord and the Rapture.

What an exciting hour that will be! Are you ready to pay the price to have your wilderness transformed?

The Voice of the Lord

One of the things the Bible says clearly about this transformation is that we will know the Lord and His glory and we will hear His voice. Before

I close this chapter, I want to tell you something very important on how to discern the voice of God, because it is through knowing His voice that we will know His power.

Acts 1:4 says that the resurrected Jesus commanded the apostles not to leave Jerusalem, but to wait for the promise of the Father which, He said, "You have heard from Me." They knew His voice before He told them they would receive the power in verse 8.

Once you know His voice, you will be led as Philip was led one day in Acts 8:26ff to go south on the desert road to Gaza where he encountered an Ethiopian eunuch in a chariot. The Spirit tells Philip to run to overtake the eunuch, which he does, and he begins talking to the man, climbs into the chariot, and listens to a passage of Scripture he is reading. When the eunuch asks what the passage means, "Philip opened his mouth, and beginning at this Scripture, preached Jesus to him" (v. 35).

The man was converted and baptized, quite simply because Philip obeyed the Spirit, and the anointing clearly came as he "opened his mouth" and "preached Jesus." Hearing and obeying the voice is central to receiving the anointing.

The anointing will come on you also as you become a witness for Jesus. As the anointing comes you must respond because, if you are not there to capture His touch, He may never pass you that way again.

Guard the anointing; cherish it. When you know

the Holy Spirit and how He moves, you will be ready in season and out of season. Sometimes He moves so very fast that it will almost make your head spin. I believe that is why Philip ran. He knew he had an opportunity to win a soul for God. At other times, the Spirit moves slowly, and you should just flow with Him, waiting for Him to take the lead.

Remember: He does not follow you; you follow Him.

You must learn how to hear His voice. Without knowing His voice, you will not know His power. As I said, the apostles, in Acts 1:4, 8, did not receive the power until they had heard the voice of their Master. Inevitably He will lead you to win souls for His kingdom.

My dear friends, in John 10:3–4, Jesus says so clearly that He will call us and lead us by name. Do you hear His voice? Jesus says His own sheep will follow Him because they know His voice. In John 10:27, Jesus repeats this important message to all believers: "My sheep hear My voice, and I know them, and they follow Me." If you claim to know Jesus, you should hear His voice and follow His lead in your life.

But there's more. We are to follow Him daily. Hear His voice daily. Psalm 95:7 challenges us that each day, today, we must listen to God's voice. The question isn't whether God is speaking to you today; it is, are you listening to Him speak to you today?

Why is it that people don't hear or listen to

a God who knows them, loves them, and desires to lead them in His peace? One reason we don't hear is because we refuse to listen. Psalm 95:8 warns us about hardening our hearts, turning against God.

You must desire to be with God to hear His voice. Fellowship with Him in prayer and worship. If you are living in sin and have not repented, you must return to Him through His grace and mercy. We must not refuse Him, as Hebrews 12:25 warns.

So, what must you do to return to His presence, to hear His voice in your life today?

First, you must withdraw from distractions. Isaiah 30:15 and 21 speak of returning in quietness and confidence, and listening to God as He directs our steps. We must pay attention to God first.

Second, as you give Him your voice in prayer, you will hear His voice in response. Remember, you will never know the voice of God without the presence of the Holy Spirit. When you withdraw from distractions and let the Spirit come upon you, God will speak.

Next, Jesus heard the voice of God because he was constantly seeking the will of God. He heard because He obeyed (John 5:30).

Finally, God calls us to hunger and thirst for righteousness (Matt. 5:6) and to pray and seek His face (2 Chron. 7:14).

Today, God is calling you to return to Him. Take a moment now to listen; I know you will hear His voice. Are you ready to know His power in your life? Be still now and let Him speak to you. Listen to Him say today, "This is the way, walk in it" (Isa. 30:21). Then you will experience His presence and power.

Chapter 15

Change Your Oil

The Bible often likens the anointing of the Holy Spirit to oil. Both can be felt and experienced. And some observations about the qualities and characteristics of oil can actually help you understand the workings of the Spirit.

For example, oil evaporates if it is not replenished regularly; it will eventually disappear. You may want to try it sometime. Pour some oil into a container and let it sit for a long time and you will find that some of it has evaporated. If enough time passes, you will find that the vessel that held the oil will be empty, with little evidence that it once held oil.

The Spirit doesn't evaporate, but you may think He has if you neglect Him that way. You must constantly allow the oil of the Spirit to flow over your life, refreshing your spiritual life. You do this through prayer, through fellowship with God, and through reading the Word of God.

The anointing will remain on your life as you

continue to walk and talk with (not always to) the Lord. When you spend time in His presence, the rich oil of the Holy Spirit will flow over your life, refreshing and renewing your spirit.

Another interesting characteristic about oil is that it leaks if there is a hole in the vessel. The hole may be tiny, or even undetectable to the naked eye, but if there is any blemish or impurity in the composition of the vessel, the oil will find it and leak out.

Ephesians 4 cautions about any potential "holes" in your vessel when it says to give no "place" to the devil. The word place derives from the Greek word for "avenue" or "window." So you are to give no avenue to the devil. Don't allow the holes of bitterness, unforgiveness, self-pity, and the like to creep into your life. For the precious oil of the Spirit will drain out.

These "holes" that attack your vessel of the Spirit are so subtle that in infancy they are difficult to detect. Bitterness can creep in almost unnoticed. And how many times have you encountered someone who is losing a lot of oil because of the holes of self-pity? All you hear from such people is "Poor, poor me."

As you seek and walk in the anointing, it is imperative that you guard against these holes and concentrate on keeping your oil fresh.

Another truth about oil is that only fresh oil has the proper density — thickness — to serve an engine or machine well. That thickness is called viscosity, and it's important, for it measures the ability of oil to withstand heat and pressure and to reduce friction or stress. The lower the viscosity, the less will the oil protect under certain levels of pressure.

As you know, it is important that you change the oil in your car regularly — so important that most auto manufacturers recommend changing the oil every three to five thousand miles to get the maximum benefit. Otherwise, in addition to getting dirty, the oil gets thin and discolored and can harm rather than protect the engine.

So also will your anointing wear thin under the heat of spiritual warfare. That is why you *must* give daily attention to prayer and Bible study. It's the only way to build and maintain your spiritual thickness and strength.

Ask Some Hard Questions

So, how fresh is your oil? Are you constantly adding fresh oil, or are you operating with an old anointing? Is God's touch on your life stale? Is it beginning to evaporate? Is your vessel cracked? Does it leak?

I know some of you are saying, "Ouch!" I hope the pain is serious enough that you will check the freshness, the level, and the strength of your anointing.

In addition to prayer and Bible study (which are indispensable), you need to listen to men and women of God. For example, I listen frequently to taped messages of Kathryn Kuhlman and read as many Christian books as I possibly can. It's important to your spiritual being and growth that you are fed by other servants of God on a regular basis.

In 2 Tim. 4:13 Paul asks Timothy to bring along the books when he visits Paul again. I can't over-emphasize the importance of learning from mature Christians. This, then, is one more way for you to be assured that your spiritual oil is regularly renewed.

Attempting to exist on yesterday's reality only brings about a slow and very deceptive form of spiritual death. There is nothing worse than to watch someone who thinks he is spiritually alive but is actually dead. The worst kind of death is dying and not recognizing that your reality has turned into rituals of religious activity.

Similarly, how often I have watched Christians who always shake and twitch, dance and shout when they worship God in song or praise. There may have been a time when God moved on them in such a powerful way that they couldn't stand still, and they may have shaken or danced or whatever. But now, it has become a religious activity or tradition derived from their early experience. When God is the author or force behind it, it is beautiful. But if it's only a religious tradition or activity — a ritual — it is the residue of former reality. It has the form of godliness, but denies its power (2 Tim. 3:5).

When your oil is fresh, it has a beautiful, fragrant aroma. But there is nothing more unpleasant than the smell of stale, rotten oil. Have you ever smelled rotten olive oil? It is repulsive.

Just as oil can smell good in the natural, so it can in the spiritual. Spiritual fragrance is definitely associated with God's people. If their lives are full of the fresh oil of the Spirit, you will detect a sweet fragrance. When the oil is stagnant and the flesh takes over, a rotten odor comes forth.

Transforming Oil

In 1 Samuel 10 you find the account of Samuel's anointing of Saul with oil. Saul was transformed. "Then the Spirit of the Lord will come upon you, and you will prophesy with them and be turned into another man," says verse 6. The anointing turns you into a different person. As I've found so powerfully at the nationwide miracle crusades, you become bold and strong. Your mind clears. Your spirit becomes sensitive. You become aware of the invisible world around you.

Yes, according to verses 6 through 9, Saul was anointed and became another man. God used him to slay thousands of Philistines. He became king over Israel.

But, tragically, flaws and holes developed. Second Samuel 1:21 tells us:

Ye mountains of Gilboa, let there be no dew, neither let there be rain, upon you, nor fields of offerings: for there the shield of the mighty is vilely cast away, the shield of Saul, as though he had not been anointed with oil. (KJV)

Warriors had special ways to care for their weapons. For example, their battle shields, made of leather, had to be rubbed with oil to preserve them. The "rubbing with oil" is symbolic of the anointing, for when our lives are rubbed with the anointing of the Holy Spirit, they become useful for the Kingdom of God. However, Saul became "as though he had not been anointed with oil." He had lost it through sin.

First Samuel 3:11-15 gives an account of Saul and his army battling the Philistines. Samuel, the judge and prophet, had promised to make certain offerings himself (10:8) before Israel went into battle. When he did not arrive as expected, Saul foolishly thought he could strengthen Israel's chances against the Philistines and offered the burnt offerings himself. With this disobedience, Saul violated God-given, fundamental standards of the offices of king and prophet. He sinned, and God looked upon him as though he had never been anointed.

After knowing the power and the intimacy of the kingly anointing, which I wrote about earlier, should you lose it, you too would lose the shield of protection, the dew, the rain of God's blessing.

After his disobedience, Saul fought the Philistines without the anointing and was soundly defeated. God called his action rebellion, likening it to the sin of witchcraft. It was filthy before God.

Furthermore, when Saul lost the kingly anointing, an evil spirit came and possessed him. The kingly anointing had given him authority over

Satan, but when he lost the anointing, the roles changed and Satan had dominion over Saul. Judas, too, you'll recall, lost the kingly anointing. Jesus had said to him and the other eleven, "Go, I give you power. Cast out devils." When Judas lost the anointing, the devil possessed him and he betrayed Jesus.

Keep Moving Forward

Once the cleansing oil of salvation has been poured out upon you and you have experienced the leper's anointing, don't stop. Press on and let the fresh oil of the priestly anointing pour over you daily, bringing you into intimate communion and fellowship with the Holy Spirit. Spend time in His presence and allow Him to fill you with Himself and His power. Then you will move to a higher plateau and enter into the kingly anointing and the accompanying power over Satan.

Guard the anointing carefully. "To whom much is given, from him much will be required" (Luke 12:48).

Remember, you can't operate on past glory, trying to survive on yesterday's oil. God's reservoir never runs dry. So don't become stagnant or complacent yourself. Invite the "oil" of the Holy Spirit to pour over you, renewing and refreshing you. For in Hebrew, the word *anoint* is *mashach*, which means "to rub in." The Greek word is *chrism* and means "to smear." Isn't that wonderful? I want the anointing to pour over me and to be rubbed in — not just on me but in me. I want that tangible anointing.

Sheep and Oil

Earlier, I mentioned "rubbing with oil" in connection with Saul and his loss of the anointing. The "rubbing," however, has other significance in Scripture. Psalm 23, one of the Bible's most beloved passages, finds David saying, "You anoint my head with oil; my cup runs over." Bearing in mind the imagery of the shepherd and his sheep, it helps to know that in the Middle East, where I was born and raised, shepherds regularly anointed their sheep with olive oil to keep insects from harassing them.

There are many bugs in the Holy Land, and the only way to give the sheep any peace from them is to rub them with oil.

For you and me, this symbolizes being kept free from the harassment of demons, by the power of the Holy Spirit. And it further establishes that Christians have the Holy Spirit in them after conversion, not demons. Rather they have the security and peace of the anointing.

The "rubbing" idea is also found in three keys to keeping and increasing the anointing. In order, the three keys are these:

First, God is always looking to see whether you are guarding what you already have. Think of the Lord's admonition to David after he had sinned with Bathsheba: "I gave you your master's house and your master's wives into your keeping, and gave you the house of Israel and Judah. And if that had been too little, I also would have given you much more! Why have you despised the commandment of the Lord, to do evil in His sight?" (2 Sam. 12:8-9). Of course, as we read in Psalm 51, David did repent and was blessed with God's renewed presence and power.

Before God gives you more, He looks to see what you've done with what He's already given.

The second key is found in Luke 24:28-31 in the account of the two men to whom the risen Christ appeared on the road to Emmaus. When they arrived at the village, Jesus indicated He was going to travel on. "But they constrained Him, saying, 'Abide with us,' " the Scripture says, and He later revealed Himself to them in the breaking of the bread. Had they not constrained Him, they would have missed a revelation.

Many people today miss the revelation of Jesus simply because they will not constrain Him, simply because they do not ask Him to abide with them. They give up too easily. He comes to them in prayer and they mistakenly think that when the presence appears to be lifting God is finished with them. The next time that happens to you, stay a little longer and constrain God not to leave right then. You'll find a revelation just beyond that point.

Third, your associations are important. Associate with anointed people because they will "rub off" on your life. They will influence you, and that will produce marvelous effects. Remember when a band of social outcasts joined David (1 Sam. 22:2)? They, too, became mighty men and giant killers as a result of their association (2 Sam. 8:18-20). The anointing on David's life had rubbed onto theirs. The same thing happened with the disciples. They received the anointing as a result of associating with the Lord Jesus (Acts 4:13). Isn't it amazing what can happen if you spend time with godly men and women?!

Do you long, even as you read this, to know the glory of His presence and the anointing of the Spirit which comes with His power? Then invite Him into your life right now. Even if you know you're saved and baptized with the Holy Spirit, say, "Holy Spirit, help me to empty myself of me so I can be filled with You. Fill me with Your presence that I may know Your power . . . that I may know Your glory . . . that I may know the precious anointing of Your Spirit."

When you learn to know His presence, His person, His glory, as He fills your being, then His power will fill your life and the anointing of His Spirit will be yours.

Chapter 16

Getting a Double Portion

How would you like to receive not only the anointing of the Holy Spirit on your life, but also a double portion of that anointing? Think of it: the presence of the Spirit each day of your life and a double measure of the power.

The story of Elijah and Elisha provide an exciting example of how double-portion power can be ours. The greatest desire of Elisha's heart was that he would receive a double portion of Elijah's anointing, and he did. We can learn from his steps of obedience that led to this marvelous gift.

Let's start by recognizing that the Old Testament's Elijah is a type of the Lord Jesus Christ, and Elisha is a type of you and me. I have found that everything in the Old Testament is a shadow, while everything you and I have received through the New Testament is the substance of that shadow. Moses, Elijah, Elisha, and the rest of the prophets walked as a type and shadow to help us see what God wants us to do and how He wants us to live.

When you read the Bible, remember that Jesus Christ is the substance of the Word of God, and the prophets who lived before He came to earth were a shadow of His substance. The prophets simply represented the substance that was to come. Another way of saying it is that the Old Testament, while absolutely true, is the shadow of the truth. The truth is Christ. So when you read the Old Testament, you should remember that you are looking at the shadow of the true substance, who lived in heaven at the time. When He came to earth, He who spoke through shadows under the Old Covenant was then substance on earth. But He who is substance always existed.

I am convinced that every detail in the Bible — Old and New Testaments — is significant, for it represents Jesus. There are no meaningless details.

Therefore, I believe it is not unrealistic for us to desire the double portion for which Elisha yearned.

Setting the Stage

First Kings 19:16 finds God giving Elijah a directive: "You shall anoint Jehu the son of Nimshi as king over Israel. And Elisha the son of Shaphat of Abel Meholah you shall anoint as prophet in your place."

The account goes on to report that, obeying the

directive, Elijah finds Elisha plowing with twelve yoke of oxen, or twenty-four oxen, which means his father, Shaphat, must have been wealthy since some of the richest men of the time only owned six oxen. So in our first encounter with the younger man, we find him dirty, sweaty, and hard at menial work, not exactly the conditions we expect for prophets. But God knew the one He wanted to finish Elijah's ministry.

The Bible says Elijah "passed by him and threw his mantle on him," which designated Elisha as his successor. Elisha, not hesitating and apparently eager to go, ran after Elijah and said, "Please let me kiss my father and my mother, and then I will follow you," showing great respect for his parents.

But then "Elisha turned back from him, and took a yoke of oxen and slaughtered them and boiled their flesh, using the oxen's equipment, and gave it to the people, and they ate. Then he arose and followed Elijah, and served him."

What does his action mean? It represents his renunciation of his former life. He left his former life and forgot it. God will never bring you to the double portion if you are carrying the weights of yesterday, which must be forgotten. Paul spoke of it as "forgetting those things which are behind and reaching forward to those things which are ahead" (Phil. 3:13). Only when you release your yesterday will you receive the promises of tomorrow.

God was not choosing a man of natural assets,

but a man of faith, who was willing to be one of the prophet's servants. Are you willing to do the same thing today with your life? It's the first step down the road to the double-portion anointing.

Now a Journey

In 2 Kings 2, we find Elijah traveling to a number of locations that I find significant and informative of where we must walk with Jesus Christ.

We find them first in Gilgal, where the cloud by day and the fire by night were no longer evident, which represents a place of religious activity with no supernatural power. It is the place where Joshua dwelled, as recorded in Joshua 5, a place where he was to forget Egypt — " 'This day I have rolled away the reproach of Egypt from you.' Therefore the name of the place is called Gilgal to this day" (Josh. 5:9).

It's the place where you forget the old life, saying, "I'm born again now; my sins are washed away. I'm having a marvelous time."

But verses ten through twelve go on to say that after keeping the Passover in Gilgal, "They did eat of the old corn of the land" (KJV).

You see, the children of Israel were dependent on God, both for their deliverance from Egypt and for their daily provision afterward. God's miraculous provision for each day was incredible. Each morning when they awoke, they found manna lying on the ground, which they would gather for

179

their needs for that day — fresh each day. However, they eventually began to take it for granted and even complain about the same old thing, despite the miraculous, loving nature of the provision. When the opportunity came, they ate the old corn, and the manna ceased the next day!

So what does this mean for us? Gilgal, in your experience and in mine, is the place we come to after our salvation experience, which is symbolized by the deliverance from Egypt. We leave our life of sin and run into the outstretched arms of our Redeemer, happy to be out of the place that held us captive for so long.

But also in Gilgal we soon forget the awfulness of our Egypt, where we needed the supernatural to get us out. Once we get comfortable and no longer seem to be dependent upon God, we see no need for the supernatural. We think we can handle things ourselves. So the manna ceases, along with the glory of God as revealed in the cloud and pillar of fire.

What, then, do I conclude from Elijah and Elisha's stop in Gilgal? As I said, Gilgal represents religion with no power. None of us really desires that at first, but that's where many of us end up. And many of us get so comfortable in Gilgal that we never leave. We're happy to be born again and satisfied with religious activity — happy with spiritual mediocrity in "the First Church of Gilgal," never growing or maturing to a double portion of God's anointing. I've talked to so many people who say things like, "If I could only feel what I felt when I got saved" or "If I could only feel the way I did when I was filled with the Spirit."

In spite of all this, there is a comforting thought. God takes you to Gilgal for a purpose: to show you that life without the supernatural is not the way the Christian life was meant to be lived.

Friends, we must go beyond Gilgal. Our attitude needs to be like Elisha's: "I'm not staying around here. I'm going beyond here to my double portion!"

On to Bethel

After Gilgal, Elijah and Elisha went to Bethel (2 Kings 2:2), which I see as a place of great decisions, a place where you can surrender and yield to God, a place of dying to your own desires. Think about it. Bethel is mentioned throughout the Old Covenant. It was the place where Abraham pitched his tent and made a decision to live for God. It was the place where his grandson, Jacob, told God he would follow and serve Him. It was the place to which he returned to fight with God and be transformed from Jacob to Israel. It was the place where Samuel first heard the voice of God. It was the place where Saul rejected the Word and lost everything, including his kingdom. Some who arrive at their Bethels succeed mightily, while others fail.

But, oddly enough, once you reach Bethel, you can surrender and yield, but you will not find your double-portion anointing there.

181

At Bethel, Elijah said to Elisha, "Stay here, please, for the Lord has sent me on to Jericho." But Elisha quickly responded, "As the Lord lives, and as your soul lives, I will not leave you!"

"No way," Elisha said. "You're not going without me. There's no double-portion anointing here. It's somewhere else, and I'm going to get it!"

You can decide to remain at Bethel or perhaps even go back to the mediocrity of Gilgal. Or you can forge ahead and enjoy the blessings of God.

Jericho, a Place of Action

Next came the place of warfare — Jericho. It was in the vicinity of Jericho that the Lord Jesus faced Satan when He was tempted for forty days and nights. It was there in Joshua's time that the walls came tumbling down.

When you arrive in Jericho, Satan will oppose you, attacking your finances, your body, your mind, your family. It's where you fight devils and all the forces of hell, but also where you will find the captain of the host. You can be certain, when you decide to sacrifice self and follow God, the devil will show up to oppose you, but the captain of the host is there with the sword ready to assist you. You can be sure that your victory is just around the corner, for warfare surrounds the birth of a miracle.

Don't Delay Your Journey

In my own Jericho, Satan tried to distract my ministry in the eighties.

I remember the pitfalls of complacency, monotony, and boredom that were right at hand. There was a dreadful risk of treating the anointing lightly. And all the time, the double-portion anointing was just around the corner, which is always the case. All I had to do was open my eyes to see the captain of the host seize the victory in the spiritual battle against diversion.

The message is simple: Don't be distracted, least of all by the flesh. Distraction is an enemy of your soul.

For example, before a miracle service the rule is that no one talks to me. I tell people, "Don't tell me anything that's happening." I don't want to know anything about anything. If I start to think about the needs of the people, my emotions get all tied up and I find it difficult to concentrate and be clearminded. I must keep my heart and mind on God, and on Him alone. I can't let Satan distract me, and you can't either. During your times of distraction, remember that God gives you the power to move on to victory.

On to the Jordan!

And so, what happens at Jordan, the next stop? God opens your eyes and you receive spiritual sight. It was at the Jordan that John the Baptist saw the Holy Spirit descending in the form of a dove. It was at the Jordan that Jesus began His ministry.

Jordan, the place where you begin to see beyond the natural and into the supernatural realm. It's the place where Elisha received his double-portion anointing. Here's a wonderful passage of Scripture;

Now Elijah took his mantle, rolled it up, and struck the water; and it was divided this way and that, so that the two of them crossed over on dry ground. And so it was, when they had crossed over, that Elijah said to Elisha, "Ask! What may I do for you, before I am taken away from you," And Elisha said, "Please let a double portion of your spirit be upon me." So he said, "You have asked a hard thing. Nevertheless, if you see me when I am taken from you, it shall be so for you; but if not, it shall not be so." Then it happened, as they continued on and talked, that suddenly a chariot of fire appeared with horses of fire, and separated the two of them; and Elijah went up by a whirlwind into heaven. Now Elisha saw it, and he cried out, "My father, my father, the chariot of Israel and its horsemen!" So he saw him no more. And he took hold of his own clothes and tore them into two pieces. He also took up the mantle of

Elijah that had fallen from him, and went back and stood by the bank of the Jordan. (2 Kings 2:8-13)

Hidden within these Scriptures is a fantastic shadow of what happens at Jordan, the place of spiritual vision. Elisha did two things. He tore off his old clothes, signifying the release of the old man and the past. Then he picked up the mantle that had fallen and knew that his double portion had come. When the new is on the way, say good-bye to the past. Give up the old so God can perform the new in your life.

You cannot receive your double-portion anointing until you know the promises of God and expect to receive them through faith in Him. Abraham had to trust God for the son He had been promised. Trusting in his own strength or in his own works did not bring the son of promise. He had to see Isaac by faith before he received him. When you see with the eyes of faith, then the promise begins to come your way with power.

Luke 18:35-43 tells of Bartimaeus, the blind man, who wore a garment traditionally worn by the blind in accordance with Hebrew custom. Anyone wearing such a garment was known to be blind and helpless, requiring assistance with the basic things in life, such as being fed and cared for. When the Lord Jesus heard him crying out, He said, "Bring him to me." Immediately Bartimaeus cast off his garment. Before he ever received his miracle, he threw off his garment, signifying his total dependence on God. He let go of the old to receive the new.

When I by faith see myself as a child of God, I no longer go with head bowed low and eyes downcast, mumbling, "Oh, God, I am so unworthy to walk in Your presence." I walk into the Holy of Holies, not with guilt, but with freedom from condemnation. The darkness that once bound me no longer clouds my spiritual eyes. I see! When I read the Word, I believe it, and I enter in as a child of God.

That is the way you are to approach the double-portion anointing.

You are not going to stay in Gilgal's mediocrity. You go on to Bethel: You'll die to self and decide for God forever. Jericho: You'll fight every devil that can come against you, and you'll win because the Lord Jesus is beside you. At Jordan, you will begin to see the promises of heaven that are yours, and you will appropriate them. You will be a force for God that will shake heaven and hell.

Chapter 17

Will You Pay the Price?

The importance of the anointing is proved in many ways, as we have seen, but no one sets it forth with more authority than the psalmist, as found in the following excerpt. Pay particular attention to the height, depth, and breadth of the promises through David to the Messiah, the ultimate Anointed One, from whom you derive your anointing:

I have found my servant David;
With My holy oil I have anointed him,
With whom My hand shall be established;
Also My arm shall strengthen him.
The enemy shall not outwit him,
Nor the son of wickedness afflict him.
I will beat down his foes before his face,
And plague those who hate him.
But My faithfulness and My mercy shall
be with him,
And in My name his horn shall be exalted.

187

Also I will set his hand over the sea,
And his right hand over the rivers.
He shall cry to Me, "You are my Father,
My God, and the rock of my salvation."
Also I will make him My firstborn,
The highest of the kings of the earth.
My mercy I will keep for him forever,
And My covenant shall stand firm with
    him.
His seed also I will make to endure forever,
And his throne as the days of heaven.

                                    (Ps. 89:20-29)

Had we nothing else but this, we should seek the wonderful gift that is ours. Strength, protection, victory over the enemy, faithfulness, authority, power, unending covenant — on and on are the promises that are yours and mine through the King of kings, the Lord Jesus.

Think About It Soberly

The anointing, which carries these promises, also carries a price, as I wrote in Chapter 1, and it is very real. You will accomplish little, or worse, should you act foolishly or insincerely.

That price is total death to self. And it comes only in prayer. Furthermore, the dying must occur daily, as Paul wrote (1 Cor. 15:31). I can't say, "But I died twenty years ago." No, the flesh must be denied daily. It is an accursed thing and must go to the cross daily. Jesus said it flat out: "If anyone desires to come after Me, let him deny himself, and take up his cross daily, and follow Me" (Luke 9:23). That comes only in prayer.

You see, you and I have no power to say no to Satan; there's no power in us to refuse him. The power only comes when the Holy Spirit is upon us. Giants of faith have fallen because they couldn't say no. They relied on their own power.

Kathryn Kuhlman said years ago, "I died a long time ago." And she could have been misunderstood unless she had gone on to say, "I die a thousand deaths," meaning that she had made the decision a long time earlier, but she had to make it again every day.

This is one of the things about the presence of the Holy Spirit. It comes quite simply by making the decision before God, saying it, meaning it, and totally abandoning yourself to Him. He knows whether you're telling the truth or not, and you'd better be aware of that.

It's a Lifetime Matter

The anointing of God, the power of God, comes upon us by spending time, and all else that is required, with Him. And it's not a one-day experience, but a lifetime, one in which you become completely sold out. I do not believe I have arrived at a 100 percent level in this, although that is truly what I desire, and God has been able to use me, especially in recent years, and He will do the same with you.

In my case, I know I have lost complete desire for anything to do with the world. My worldly desires are gone.

It's hard to talk about these things and sound truthful in our cynical age, but because of the presence and the anointing of the Spirit, I am consumed by my walk and work with God. He is literally all I have. If He said, "Benny, move to China," I'd leave everything and go. I no longer have any rebellion in me.

The lack of material desire does not mean that Satan has stopped tempting me. The daily death to self, often very difficult, is still a battle that must be fought.

A Candid Question

A good friend asked a question that gave me pause recently. "Do you think God has used you the way He has," he asked, "because you were such a loner and so withdrawn that you didn't have much to die to when you were young?"

He raised an important point, as I thought about it. I had an awful speech impediment, I was little, and I was terribly shy. I would often hide under my bed when visitors came to our home.

But when God began to use me, I basically had nothing to lose, and I wasn't tied to anything. I had certain desires, naturally, as every human being has — certain things I wanted. But God dealt with me on those.

So, after considering the question seriously, I believe God often chooses people like me, who He knows aren't going to fight Him. But then, there is the absolute truth that when you are in God's presence and tasting His goodness and His love, you say, "Who wants anything else?" He just consumes you. I've found that as you try to explain this to people and tell them what they're missing, they often look at you as though you're crazy.

The amazing thing is that He loves you so much, and yet you're not always right with Him. I mess up, and I miss the mark so often, and I grieve Him so often, but never intentionally. I would rather die than that. I love Him too much to hurt Him like that. But when I do miss, He gently comes and deals with me on my sins and failures and weaknesses, and I go on, forgiven.

My friend asked an even harder question about my commitment to the ministry, but the answer was easier. "Are you sure you don't love the work of the Lord simply because you're good at it?" he asked, implying: ". . . and there's not much else you could do?"

I have examined my heart many times and immediately concluded that I would never ruin my life and my family's life serving something and killing my relationship with God. It sounds heroic, but it's as Paul said, the love of God constrains me (2 Cor. 5:14).

I have a chance to see God's incredible love for people. When I stand on that platform at a miracle crusade and see the thousands of people, the kids, and the wheelchairs, the souls of men and women hungry for their Creator, I know exactly why I'm in the ministry. I pray every time, "Help me pay a higher price to see them touched."

And I have to say, I don't know why every person isn't touched and healed, but I do know that thousands upon thousands are. And I also know that the full answer lies in the anointing of the Holy Spirit and the desire we have for Him — the willingness we have to pay the price.

And I am confident that thousands of you will be willing to pay that price too. God still loves the world and its people more than we'll ever be able to imagine.

Much Respect is Required

In addition to the price we must pay for the presence and the anointing of the Holy Spirit, there is the important matter of respect for that anointing. It may not sound terribly spiritual, but I have heard God warn about "playing games" with the anointing. And I urge you, as you move forward in the life with the Spirit, do not allow anything that would be disrespectful to the Lord.

Warning against disrespect for the obvious anointing of the Spirit came early in the history of God's dealing with Israel. Numbers 12 opens by saying that Miriam and Aaron spoke against Moses because of the Ethiopian woman Moses had married.

They challenged Moses with these words: "Has the LORD indeed spoken only through Moses? Has He not spoken through us also?" (vs. 2). And here the Scripture says parenthetically that Moses was more humble than all men on the face of the earth. He was God's chosen man, and God judged them for their disrespect.

Moses "is faithful in all My house. I speak with him face to face, even plainly, and not in dark sayings," God said. "Why then were you not afraid to speak against My servant Moses? (vs. 7-8)"

God did not like their disrespect for Moses and his anointing, the Bible says, "So the anger of the Lord was aroused against them, and He departed. And when the cloud departed from above the tabernacle, suddenly Miriam became leprous, as white as snow."

God's displeasure was strong, and had it not been for Moses' intervention with God, Miriam would have remained "as one dead." Aaron apologized and pleaded, and Moses cried to God, "Please heal her, O God, I pray!" So God let her stay in punishment for seven days, shut out of the camp, and then she was healed (vs. 11-15).

The point is: Aaron and Miriam walked away from their callings and tried to be a Moses, despising the powerful anointing upon him. Never try to be a Moses if you are not. And it is beneficial to notice that the cloud lifted before the leprosy hit. People who walk away from their anointing will realize sooner or later that the presence is gone. Yes, God will forgive them when there is repentance, but there is still a price to pay.

The Horse and Mule

As you prepare to surrender to the Holy Spirit, dying to yourself, and moving into the marvelous presence and anointing He has for you, I want to share one verse of Scripture that can be a pointed needle in your side. I know it has often provided a rebuke for me.

Psalm 32:9 says, "Do not be like the horse or like the mule, which have no understanding, which must be harnessed with bit and bridle."

Think of it. One day the Lord gave me that verse, and the Holy Spirit literally shook me up with it.

Do you know what a horse does? He runs ahead and is impatient. What about a mule? He is so stubborn he won't move. One runs too fast, and the other won't run at all.

The serious message is that the horse will run out of the anointing and into the flesh, while the mule dies in the flesh. Sadly there are a lot of mules in the church. They don't want anything from God, no presence, no anointing. They are stubborn.

If I can't have all sheep, who will follow the Lord faithfully, then I would rather have horses in my church than mules. At least horses are going somewhere, and you have a chance at bringing them under control.

194

It's Time to Move

As I said earlier, these are powerful times in which we live. Sin abounds, but grace does much more abound. Millions of people, unhappily, are charging in the opposite direction from God. Society is in a shambles. Our young people are suffering. But other millions are hungry for God and want to line up with Him and serve Him. I trust you are in the latter group, and I pray that as you go forward, you will go forward in the power of the Holy Spirit, in His precious anointing that is for all of God's people.

Let nothing deter you. He wants you so very badly.

Please pray with me:

Father, I surrender to You completely now. I yield everything to You — my body, my soul, and my spirit, my family, my job, my finances, my weaknesses, my strengths, my past, my present, and my future, everything I am, for all eternity. I ask You, Lord, to give me a repentant heart for all the things I've done to grieve You, all my sins, my iniquities, my coldness of heart, and my lack of trust. I ask You to empower me to turn around, to go the other way, the way that pleases You. Holy Spirit, I welcome You into my life right now. I praise You and love You. I ask You to help me receive the things I've asked for from the Father through Jesus. Help me to come into fellowship and communion with You, for I really don't know how to myself. Make me fully aware of Your presence and enable me to hear Your voice. I promise to obey. Lord Jesus, anoint me with the Holy Spirit as I obey and learn. Give me Your power to touch those around me and those You will bring across my path. Show me what to do next. And help me never to neglect Your fellowship. I pray in the name of Jesus my Lord. Amen.

I will put My Spirit within you and cause you to walk in My statutes, and you will keep My judgments and do them. (Ezek. 36:27)

But you shall receive power when the Holy Spirit has come upon you; and you shall be witnesses to Me in Jerusalem, and in all Judea and Samaria, and to the end of the earth. (Acts 1:8)